CLOSE TO THE EARTH

CLOSE TO THE EARTH

Living Social History of the British Isles

JUDITH COOK

ROUTLEDGE & KEGAN PAUL

LONDON, BOSTON, MELBOURNE AND HENLEY

First published in 1984
by Routledge & Kegan Paul plc

14 Leicester Square, London WC2H 7PH, England

9 Park Street, Boston, Mass. 02108, USA

464 St Kilda Road, Melbourne,
Victoria 3004, Australia and

Broadway House, Newtown Road,
Henley-on-Thames, Oxon RG9 1EN, England

Set in Palatino by Columns
and printed in Great Britain
by T.J. Press (Padstow) Ltd, Padstow, Cornwall

Library of Congress Cataloging in Publication Data

Cook, Judith.
Close to the earth.
Bibliography: p.
1. Great Britain – Social conditions. 2. Miners – Great
Britain. 3. Fishermen – Great Britain. 4. Farmers – Great
Britain. I. Title.
HN385.C616   1984   306'.0941   84-6819

British Library CIP data available

ISBN 0-7100-9634-8

FOR MY CHILDREN

CONTENTS

LIST OF PLATES

ACKNOWLEDGMENTS

A great many people made this book possible. First I would like to thank all those who gave up a considerable amount of time to talk to me. I would like to thank Mrs Phyllis Pawlyn of Newlyn for permission to use James Hosking's diary and the Sanders family of Baddesley for letting me use that of William Sanders. My thanks to the Penders of Mousehole for all their help and permission to use the memories of Mrs Nettie Pender. I would like to thank the Reverend Hugh Alexander for introducing me to Mr Jack Down without whom the book would not have been complete. My thanks to the County Archivist, County Records Office, Truro, the management of Baddesley Colliery, Young's Brewery and the staff of *The Landworker*.

The author and publishers are grateful to the following for permission to reproduce plates: Plates 1, 2, 3, 13, 15, 16, 17 and 18, pictures by kind permission of Mr Reg Watkiss; for Plates 4, 5, 6, 7, 8, 9 and 10 we acknowledge the assistance of the West Midlands Region of the National Coal Board (plates donated by Reverend F.W. Cobb); Plates 11 and 12, Gwynedd Archives Service; Plates 14, 24 and 25, The Suffolk Record Office; Plates 19 and 20, The National Museum of Wales (Welsh Folk Museum); Plates 21 and 22, F. Gibson, Isles of Scilly; Plates 23, 27 and 28, Warwick County Record Office; Plates 26 and 31, courtesy of the Bedford Archive; Plates 29 and 30, The Shakespeare Centre; Plates 32 and 33, Young's Brewery, Wandsworth.

INTRODUCTION

This is a book I have wanted to write for a very long time. I suppose the idea first came years ago when a Cornish painter, Jack Pender (whose mother and father are featured in the book) and I were talking about the massive changes he and I had seen in Cornwall just in our own lifetimes. We had been laughing wryly about the traditional 'Cornish Sunday' back in our grandparents' day and then went on to exchange stories we had heard from old people when we were young. I felt then that somebody somewhere ought to write down some of the memories of a way of life which was disappearing within a generation, before even the memory of it no longer remained.

Journalism and other problems intervened in the meantime but there has now been a definite move to try and record some of our living social history before it entirely disappears into the past. Then I was given the chance to realise my ambition.

Obviously one could have written a book four times the size – there was no shortage of subject matter. What I felt was necessary was to sort out some kind of scheme in my own mind and then follow that.

I decided, therefore, to divide the book into three sections with one interlinking piece. In *Out of the Earth* I have looked at what literally does come out of the earth – stone, tin, coal and slate. The stonemason, Mervyn Williams from Llandeilo in West Wales, not only spoke about his craft but could recall the days when that small market town was a very different community.

There is some small activity in the tin mining industry in Cornwall now but nothing like the great days. Raymond Harry was one of the last of the old Cornish miners and he spoke to me about his memories nearly fifteen years ago. (That was before I thought of recalling them elsewhere but it seemed a pity to let them go.) For the diary of James Hosking I am indebted to Mrs Phyllis Pawlyn of Newlyn in Cornwall whose family paper it was. It is an almost unique account of tin mining in the days of the last great upsurge in the industry, towards the end of the nineteenth century, and also of life on a small croft. My father was a miner at Baddesley Colliery in Warwickshire and the two old miners interviewed were friends of his — both have died recently. The account of the colliery disaster was taken from first-hand accounts at the time and, again, from a diary still kept by the family of the man who wrote it, William Sanders.

Len Owens of Blaenau Festiniog completed this section with one of the grimmest stories of conditions in an industry and of the lives of those who were entirely dependent on it.

With 'Coastal waters' and fishing I turned first to the area I know best — the Cornish coast and estuaries. Jack Pender's parents (his mother, Nettie, is now dead) produced lively reminiscences going back a century and John Jack, along with records from the local newspaper, gave me the lovely story of the Great Newlyn Fishing Battle, the apotheosis of the Cornish Sunday. The battle was fought between the Newlyn men and those from Lowestoft so it was to Lowestoft I turned next where, fortunately, I had already worked on a film some years ago for Anglia Television on the old days of the herring fishing and where I first met the net maker, Jessie Thacker.

'Oysters is a mystery' says Henry Merrifield, from the River Fal, so it seemed a good idea to find out something about them and the only free oyster fishery left in Great Britain. Also fast dying away is the craft of coracle fishing, only a handful of boats still work on the rivers of West Wales and I feel fortunate to have seen them fishing. Ocky Owen of Llanstephan could remember a time when that tiny town was a thriving holiday resort and his story is sad, sad for a way of life that has passed and even sadder for what man's greed has done to the cockle fishers. Greed has almost destroyed our fishing industry.

To make a link between the coastal people and those who work the land I went back to one of my favourite places, the Isles of Scilly. For many years − and I first visited the islands as a child − the island way of life remained remarkably untouched and such holidaymakers as visited them came just for that reason. Change really began about fifteen years ago but it has accelerated out of all belief in the last two or three years, deeply upsetting most of those islanders who still remain − many can no longer afford to live there. Criticism of what has happened draws down on one, as I discovered when I wrote a piece about it in the *Guardian*, massive abuse from those few natives who think all change is for the best and from the hoteliers and entrepreneurs who have moved in to the islands in a big way. Suffice it to say that few remain who can recall that old way of life and that within a few years I believe there will be nobody left to record any of it.

Moving to the land there is 94-year-old Edith Breedon, farmer's wife on a very big Warwickshire farm, George Crisp, who spent a lifetime as a farm worker in Suffolk and the splendid Lilly Digweed, whose husband supplemented his poor farmworker's earnings by being the area's finest poacher. . . . Jack Down also farmed but in an area as different from the lush fields of Warwickshire and the estuaries of Suffolk as you can imagine − his story begins on Dartmoor nearly eighty years ago. Finally I have rounded the book off with an account of life in a totally different kind of village, a London 'village'. Yet for those who worked for Young's Brewery in Wandsworth, particularly before the last war, it was a village within the city where most of the employees lived within walking distance of the brewery and the brewery provided the main employment for the area. It is reassuring when most things change to know that this brewery still brews its beer in the way beer has been brewed for centuries and sees no reason to change.

I have come into contact with marvellous people in the course of researching the book. All the older men and women had the most stunning memories − every little detail of past events could be lovingly recalled. It became very difficult. As I spoke over a period of time to each one I kept thinking that this *must* be the best, only to think the same thing again with the next one.

Reading the diaries too of James Hosking and William Sanders, in their immaculate script, was both moving and exciting.

I have not tried in any way to idealise these accounts. No one reading any of them can be under any illusion that life for all of them was very hard. None of these workers in stone or coal, fishers of the sea or workers of the land had an easy time of it and plenty of money at the end of the day. But what does shine through is that all of them, apart from those who worked in the private coal mines and in the slate, feel that life back at the beginning of the century was better than it is now.

It is not just a question of looking backwards and it appearing that way now; it would seem that in some ways it was true. All of them say how much kinder and more caring family and neighbours were – they had to be. Treats and social gatherings were rarer and therefore more valued. There was no television to do away with conversation or evening and weekend activity so people mixed with each other more to make their own fun and entertainment. In some country areas people are much more cut off now than they ever were – fifty years ago there were railways running through many villages and linking them to the towns, carriers' carts plying regularly into the next town. Now there is not even a post office or a village bus.

Life was not only hard but dangerous. Those working in the tin and coal mines knew that they might die underground at any time – the first-hand accounts of the disasters at the Levant tin mine in Cornwall and Baddesley Colliery are the spectacular side of that fear; many other miners just died singly. Slate workers faced early death from disease. For those at sea, death was an ever-present peril and nowadays it takes something like the Penlee lifeboat disaster, of Christmas 1981, to spell out that man has not tamed the ocean.

Disease, too, took its toll – diphtheria still carried off babies and tuberculosis was rife in the mining villages. But the whole nation did not live under the threat of annihilation as we do now, who live under the shadow of the hydrogen bomb. Nobody accepted a viewpoint that man had the right to end the world and all life on it at a moment's notice. That, perhaps most of all, gave a feeling of continuity we no longer can achieve.

The industrial revolution began the time of great change, the mass production line and the desire for consumer goods accelerated it. Now we find ourselves in a position where that peak has passed and, having destroyed so many of the smaller crafts and industries in its wake, has left nothing whatsoever in their place except derelict factories and millions of unemployed. It is not a happy picture.

There must have been thousands of old people who had wonderful stories to tell from the past that have gone to their graves unrecorded. I hope here to have properly recorded the memories of a few of them and that they will appeal to others as they have appealed to me. I have also, where necessary, supplemented their accounts with those of much younger people − such as Captain James Whitehouse, Truro harbourmaster − when it seemed necessary.

For me, at least, their memories have become mine.

PART 1

OUT OF THE EARTH

1

The oldest craft

Mervyn Williams — stone mason

If I were casting a film or a play and wanted a man who entirely fitted my own image of Merlin, the wizard, then I would choose Mervyn Williams of Llandeilo in Dyfed. He is small, merry, a true Celt and has not only a lively wit but combines this with a mystical sense of the past.

Like Owen Glendower in Shakespeare's *Henry IV Part I* I could visualise him calling spirits from the vasty deep.

Llandeilo is a small market town which lies in the fertile Towy valley in West Wales. The Brecon Beacons, crowned by Pen-y-Fan, rear up to the south, while to the north, the hills climb away towards the coast. The town itself hangs on the side of a steep hill rather like the French small towns and villages of the Dordogne. At the lower end of the valley is the Ammanford coalfield, an anthracite field which is considered to produce the best quality coal in the British Isles.

However, local and rural industries have declined along with the population, leaving Llandeilo itself dwindling in importance, its big markets long gone, its tannery, brewery and small industries vanished. It has become a place through which the holiday visitors pass quickly on their way to the ferries in Fishguard or, in the other direction, to the modern shopping centre and the port of Swansea. Those from outside who stay are the walkers and the salmon fishermen – the Towy river is rich in both salmon and sewin, salmon trout.

Mervyn Williams's family has been cutting stone in Llandeilo for longer than anyone can remember. No doubt a Williams was cutting granite for local bridges back in the sixteenth century when the Penders, who feature in the chapter on west country fishing, were fighting the Spaniards in Mousehole in 1592.

Although he has technically retired he is always being called in when people have problems with stone from how best to build an archway to how to cut lettering on a difficult surface. Although he says that he had not intended to become a mason he has marvellous hands for it, large and rugged for his small frame and with fine, flexible fingers. He can pick up any piece of rock or stone and tell you its history, its use and how it should be treated.

His house stands foursquare in the one main street of the little town, built of stone and double fronted. Its immaculate interior is full of furniture and objects lovingly collected by Mervyn and his wife over the years, a beautiful corner cupboard, a magnificent dresser loaded with fine pottery. He has the old Welsh gift of story telling which holds the listener right the way through, reserving the punch for the end.

He loves his town and he loves his craft. Llandeilo did not depend on stone in the way Mousehole or Newlyn did on fishing or the fertile villages of Warwickshire on the farms, but masonry was one of the many interlinked small industries which helped to keep the town thriving, the demise of which has hastened its decay, as Mervyn will tell you.

'Now let me tell you first about the town. It was the financial centre for the whole area – there were four big Banks here. Now what happened in the last century which changed everything for good was the coming of industry.

'The coal was here, it started 5 miles away at Llandybie, and it opened up the whole valley. Soon there was nothing to be seen but small mines for miles around, along with tin plate works and such industries. That was a really big change. People don't realise, you know.

'A man said to me one day, "you know, they never grew

corn here, you can tell" and I said rubbish! He asked me why I said that — there was quite obviously nothing around here to show there had ever been corn grown as a regular crop and I told him that when I was a boy I'd actually counted up and there had been 10 or 12 mills just between here and Bethlehem (about 4 miles away), *water* mills for grinding *corn* and surely nobody went to all that trouble to build a water mill if they'd nothing to grind, did they? It was a very expensive thing to build and it was also a very profitable thing.

'The miller's pig was always the fattest pig. So much stuff came surplus to requirements that it went to feed the pig. Only after that did they open up the valley and manpower was wanted and building was wanted and labour was wanted and the farming community that had collected the money was coming now to invest it. Money was pouring in. Now there was an old lawyer in Llandeilo and they'd come to him from Llandybie and Pen-y-groes and they wanted to build a house and to get a mortgage — there were no building societies and they'd come to arrange to get some cash and he'd say he could arrange it and he'd make the mortgage and charge them for that, then he'd charge the farmers for finding the place and collecting the interest for them, then he made money on all the transactions and he died a very rich man. He was only 59 and my father made his tombstone and he had cut on it, "Work while it is yet day for the night cometh when no man can work. . . ." When you cut words in stone you find there's no occasion in life for which there isn't a text somewhere in the Bible.

'The people drifted down to the coalfield from the country-side, from Carmarthenshire and Cardiganshire, looking for work. I remember as a boy meeting a man and he was a second servant man to a big house in Cardiganshire and he got £3 a quarter and his keep and the top man was getting £7 a quarter. Well he came to work in Brynammon and he was cutting the hard headings, cutting the channels down to get to the coal and he was earning then unheard of wages — he was earning up to £7 a week on a good week. He said his mother was there at night praying for John down there with the rats and the water in the cold under the mountain and praying he would come back home but he never did. There was never enough money in the country and that's how it was.

'He came to Llandeilo and married and built a house and never went back and that happened all the time. They denuded the countryside of the cheap agricultural labour and about the same time the cheap American corn came in and that finished the local corn growing. In every village the first thing in the morning you heard and saw was the sound of the anvil and the smoke from the blacksmith's shop.

'At the end of the day the lads would all be bringing in the horses to be shod and there was a competition then as to who could strike hardest and the old blacksmith would get paid for nothing then and it was the centre of conversation and "had you heard?" and "who's who?" It was the meeting place for all the chat, the Llandeilo blacksmith's.

'Then there were the furniture makers. When a son was born if a family could afford it then they would buy a tree for him and have it cut down and properly weathered. It was usually oak. Then when he came to marry then the village carpenter or the town carpenter here would make furniture for him, most probably a dresser and a table and a corner cupboard. Behind where I live now they made the most magnificent wooden carriages you've ever seen and across from the carpenters was old Davy Stevens the blacksmith.

'I asked him once how to make a spring, how to temper it. "Well," he said. "I shouldn't tell you. I know you're a good boy in the forge and can temper the tools and twist the railings but you're a mason not a blacksmith," then he said perhaps he'd show me since probably no one would make them again and he told me how to temper a spring in the fire and I made a spring, as a boy, for my cart. It was a proper leaf spring as the old man showed me and that was all done by judgment, that was judgment by colour as you put it in the water and knowing when to stop it when the heat was running down and knowing when to de-temper it. It was like tempering our tools, letting the heat get too much and then bringing them back to the colour we wanted.

'I wanted to leave school when I was 14 and my Dad gave me a damn good thrashing and sent me back. I'd to stay on 'til I was 15. My brother Jack had been going to carry on in the business but he died when he was young and that was that so

I came out of school into the stone. That meant I'd to work with the men. My father and uncle owned the place but I'd to learn my craft as a mason with the men under a wonderful man called George Howell. He looked exactly like Jesus Christ in the picture books with the beard and that and he really was a gentleman.

'He wasn't Welsh. He'd come from Hastings, I believe. He always said he'd go back but never did. A holiday would come and he'd go on the booze and that was that. I was taught by him.

'In those days men would arrive, they'd call them travelling masons. We knew most of them and would give them work but sometimes one would come and you didn't know him so you'd say what kind of mason are you and they'd say perhaps they were a "banker mason", that's a mason who would cut the stone on which you were to work. You never asked a mason's name — oh no. It was strictly forbidden. Half of them had run away and left their wives but having the craft in their hands they could go where they liked. You'd say what shall we call you? They'd say, George or Dick or something and of course there were no insurance cards. You weren't traceable like you are today.

'So to see what kind of a craftsman they were we'd put the tools out all ready for them. We never asked for credentials but the way a man sharpened his tools, spat on the tools and sharpened them told us everything. We knew. One of the first things I learned about was tools. George would say "go to the forge and sharpen the tools" and I'd to do that and also temper them. Every stone has to have a separate temper or it won't bite. A stone tempered for granite, say, won't touch marble. It won't bite. Then if you tempered it for marble and tried to cut granite it would crumple up, it would be too soft. You had to take the steel — ordinary steel — to the hardest temper you could without it flaking. You saw little black spots in it when you got it right.

'Then you got your hammer, mallet, straight edge, rule and then if ever you tell this to a masonic gentlemen you will know what next. . . . You made your apron. Then you worked for the master of the lodge. I wouldn't have picked a tool up without his permission. He'd say "boy, temper that again, it flaked" then he'd set you off on something simple, a couple of ends and a curve and so on. We made everything then. We used to go to the Forest of Dean to get stone, "s to s", sawn two sides. That was the memorial stone came from there. Then we'd other kinds of stone — for houses, arches, bridges, we'd so much church work too.

'My uncle was a master mason. He'd bring in a stone for cutting and he was a boy! He'd go to any extremes to avoid cutting off anything from that old stone. He'd square it up and trim it and shape it and it didn't make any difference if it had been 3 inches shorter, he wasn't working to any standard but you see he couldn't bear any waste. Waste was the thing. Then he'd get us to put it on edge and he'd work on it. Then he'd call, "Tom, Mervyn, Willie! Turn the stone!", and we'd come and give the stone a turn and brush off the dust and continue but he wouldn't raise the stone himself or turn it or pick up a shovel or a wheelbarrow, no. He'd brush his own work and rub the mouldings — he'd never let anyone touch that, but everything else was for the labourers and he was a master mason. He was right about the mouldings, they might get the mitreing wrong or rub it wrong. That was all part of the craft. Then perhaps he'd pass it on to Luke the Carver. He was a Scotsman and I asked him why he was in Wales and he said one night he'd got drunk and gone back home and there was his wife with eight kids and another one expected and "she started shouting at me so I picked up my tools and I walked out and I never went back".

'Wasn't it lovely then, though, when you could pick up your craft, put it in your bag, hoist it on your shoulder and off you'd go? No one asked who you were or what you were, you were judged on what you could do. Old as I am I was standing in Wells Cathedral one day looking at some stone and touching it and a chap came up and said, "you look as if you are interested," and I said, "I'm a stone cutter, a letter cutter and a carver, any chance of a job?" He said, "Good God man, you could start tomorrow. We'd have a mason at last."

'You see when I started the craft had come down in a continuous line. Take this saw. It consisted of a cross piece, an iron blade and a mode of tightening it. It was suspended over a pulley and another pulley to counterweight it. We'd go up the mountain and get the white silica sand and we'd put a plate under it, a bit of slate, and we'd get a vessel with a little tap to give it a little drip of water and we'd mark with the tool where it would go and we'd be off. There would be old Owen Richards sawing away, back and forth. It was floating more or less. Someone once told me that in Aberdeen gaol the convicts were put six to a saw and it didn't matter how slow it went, it wasn't supposed to stop. They were in for life so there was no hurry. They used to saw granite there, six to a saw!

'One man could work our old saw. One day I went to the British Museum and there in an old picture was an Egyptian and he was sawing and I shouted out, "Look, look — there's our saw!" There was the damn old thing four thousand years old and it had never changed. Instead of a pulley they'd floated it on a tree, a sapling they'd bent over, but the rest was just the same and there was the old chap sawing. We've come back in a circle now to where we started before that — still sawing stone with another stone, though the stone's now a diamond.

'But just before the war my Dad decided to modernise and he broke the old saw up. He'd not done it a fortnight when three men arrived from Yorkshire who had a museum or something and they'd heard we had this old saw. Where was it? Oh, I said, my Dad had lit the fire with it! What was remarkable was that the blade of the saw was iron. Steel would have been no good. It was the sand that did the cutting but the best thing of all would have been copper or bronze and the Egyptians had them. You sawed away and fed it with water and sand in the middle and the slurry came out each end.

'So how did we cut the stone in the big blocks in the first place? You see we'd cut a vee, like a saw tooth upside down, and then we'd put what we called feathers in, that's two bits of metal old bed laths we'd use very often, then we'd put the wedges in between, steel wedges, then we'd start tapping them — ting, tang, tong, tung, ting, tang, then up to ting, t-ing, t-i-n-g, the highest note you could, then we'd pour in water. Now you can't compress water. So do you realise what we were cutting that stone with? Supersonic sound. The vibration was going down and the higher the note the higher the frequency per second and the vibration was going through that stone and the water couldn't be compressed and it was splitting beautifully. Do you know once I found a slug in the middle of a huge block and that slug was alive? There was nothing for it to eat, no way it could have got there yet it is impossible to think it got in there with the sedimentary rocks, before compression by the heat. I should have put it in a bottle and preserved it.

'It's a craft but it's a dying craft and there's nothing left. When they said Michael Angelo carved such and such that was nonsense. He may have designed it and he may have finished it but he never worked it all for it was the same principle. The last boy in did the roughest work, shaping, then the travelling man would do his bit, then the craftsman would take it a bit further, then the carvers would do their bit, then the letter cutters and finally the man himself would come in and do the finishing, though he'd have supervised it all, of course.

'No one wants to do it. I wrote to Scotland where they used to do fine work in granite because I wanted something done and they said, "Mr Williams, you must be an optimist, we've not a single mason who could cut or polish it working here today. Anything we can machine out we can do but when it comes to hand work, it's finished." It is very, very sad.

'When you look back at the great works in stone you must remember that time was of no consequence, and there was plenty of labour.

'But the craft goes back longer even than the old saw. My father and I were working on cutting the stone for the bridge at Fairfach when old Evans came by and he said to me, "you boys know everything, look and tell me what's this?", and it was a piece of stone with a hole in it. He said, "what was that for and how could they bore a hole through it like that?" I said to him now I'll ask *you* a question, why did they bore the hole? Now remember man was born into a world of coldness, wild animals and bones. He doesn't have iron or bronze, he doesn't have anything. So why did he go to the trouble of boring that hole and making that fine stone?

'Oh, said old Evans, perhaps it was for the loom. The loom, I said, the loom wasn't coming for thousands of years. That stone was a man's whole fortune in existence, and they buried it with him for the hereafter. So tell me, boy, he said what was it and how did they do it?

'Now I think that all those thousands of years ago someone like my great grandfather that far back sat at the mouth of the cave and he had these ideas and his wife was going at him about sitting there with his ideas while her sister's husband, the great hunter, was out getting sabre tooth tiger skins and meat and so on while all she had was rabbit and he said to her, "My dear, one day, you'll have all the sabre tooth tigerskins you could wish."

'Then one day he shouts, "I've got it" and they all crowd round and he's made this stone. It was a tedious job but he'd got it right. He got a sharpish stone and chipped it then he put it on another piece of stone and he rubbed them together, like two inverted saucers and he wondered how to bore a hole through it. Then it came to him — and we still bore holes in stones in the same way. He got a bone — his mother-in-law's leg I think it was — and filled it up with sand and he started turning it and exactly the same as sawing the stone, the sand was cutting it and only cutting the core. The core was coming up through, so he was only cutting the channel the width of the bone. Then he turned it over and bored this way. Whenever you see these things you find the hole is never absolutely parallel because he couldn't hold it parallel.

'So why did he do it — stone axes, stone hammers? No. He then puts a bit of stick in it, and before that he tests it to see he got it level and to do that he puts a bit of water on it and he twists it 'til it's level, then in goes the stick and the flywheel fell and he rubbed that until it fell beautifully back. Then he puts a thong on the stick and a bow and he goes zzzzzzzzzzz with it — and he's got fire.

'He's taken the power of God and the power of heat from the sun and he now can make fire, whenever he wants it. Now everyone wants them so he's turning them out tediously and he thinks what am I doing this for and gets the boys out turning the bones and then you've got an industry. Then you've got the craft and the mystery and no one was allowed in that cave except the stone cutters. The boys would be chipping and the young men boring and cutting and the mason's wife, she'd sabretooth tiger skins to spare and an elephant skin to sleep on and she was really *casual* about it by then because she was the wife of the first mason. Now he's started an industry, next commerce. He can't hunt tigers, he can work stone so he barters his stones for other things. The apprentices come from far and wide and are sworn to secrecy.

'He has taken the power of the sun. He has invented the flywheel. He has made the reciprocating mass into a rotary mass and an engine couldn't go without it. He has made the pendulum. And that night he looks out of the mouth of the cave at the setting sun and he *knew*. He'd worn the shadow of the mantle of the power of God, the power of the sun, and that night man set out on his journey to the stars or the dark road to the long night of oblivion and the atomic bomb. He had turned mechanical power into heat. Generations later man would turn heat into mechanical power.

'He was the great grandfather of all the masons. He was probably here in the Towy valley too, he couldn't have found that stone anywhere else.

'On his way through the generations, the mason did all kinds of other things of course. He was a carver. Look at the stone heads in the churches and cathedrals. These were the ordinary people of the town. There's always an evil, ugly fellow and that would have been the foreman. It was like people being pleased at being photographed for the local paper. They'd always stand for the masons, pretty girls, old wives, the market women who came when the market was all round the church or cathedral, the horse dealers, the loafers, the old drunks who'd be happy to have a penny or two for standing around. It wasn't like the Greeks — they carved to an idea not to a person. These were the ordinary people of the time.'

Apart from war service, Mervyn has spent all his life in the valley and for him it is a very mystical place.

'One night as a very young man I was coming back from Swansea over the mountain road and it was foggy and I lost my way. I came to this building and leaning over the gate was a man in a funny kind of three-cornered hat. I asked him the way to Llandeilo — I was on my bicycle — and he answered me in Welsh and showed me where to go. I was so grateful I got

6d. out and pressed it into his hand for a drink — and it fell
straight through the ground. I got on my bike and I went down
the road so fast I came off at the next bend. Years and years
later they drained an old pond from by the building — it had
been a tannery — and there they found a skeleton covered in
old skin, tanned like hide with the tannin in the water — and it
was wearing a three-cornered hat. . . .

'But you should have seen Llandeilo in the old days, it was a
busy, busy place. Just opposite was the old brewery. I
remember once they'd a brew went wrong and they opened
the taps and let it all run away. The people came running —
they threw the slops out, they threw the pig food out, they
threw the washing out, and the coal out and they came with
anything that would hold liquid and with the buckets and the
pans and caught it, and then out came the pokers red hot from
the fire and "hiss, hiss" into the beer it went and there you had
mulled beer. No one went to work for a fortnight, they were so
drunk they couldn't walk. They've pulled it down. It was
started with £5000 of capital and I have my uncle's shares in it.

'There was an old mason one night went down home to
Fairfach and he'd bought sausages cheap. It was Saturday and
they had to sell everything off in those days, there was no
fridges. Well he'd been on the toot and he was staggering
home with the sausages around his neck and along comes a
man in a horse and trap and knocks him down. The man feels
the body and feels the sausages and thinks, "My God, I've
killed him," and he pressed a golden guinea in the old mason's
hand and ran away. Up he sits and there he is with the
sausages round his neck and a golden guinea in his hand as
well.

'Llandeilo was full of characters when I was a boy. There
was a lawyer we called Jimmy Genteel, because he was a bit
above us all. One day a man came in the White Horse with a
leg of lamb and he put it down and it got eaten by a dog. He
enquired around and found the dog was Jimmy Genteel's so
off he went to call on Jimmy. "Oh," he says to Jimmy, "a man
took a drink with his friends and while he was doing so, he
put his meat down and a dog took it, now could he claim on
the dog's owner?" "Oh yes," said the lawyer, "and do you
know whose dog it was?" "Well, sir," said the man, "it's

yours." "How much did you say you spent on the meat — 3s. 6d? How the working classes can afford such extravagance, I don't know!" But he paid him 3s. 6d., and the man said thank you and the lawyer said, "Wait a minute. You owe me 4s. You'd asked my advice and you didn't say it was my dog, just asked what the law was and I told you so, that costs you 7s. 6d., and that, less the 3s. 6d., means you owe me 4s." That's a true story.

'Twice a year there was the big fair in Llandeilo. They came in from the country farms and from the collieries and they all spent their money in the town. There was no shops in the countryside then, so they came to Llandeilo and the shops and the market as the shopping centre. They'd come in on the little train. There was so many of them you could have walked on their heads coming up from the station.

'Now old James who lived up the bank, he'd a very tight wife. So he nicked two half-crowns when she wasn't looking and went to the churchyard and he put them under the sundial in the yard, intending later when he could get away from his wife to come out for a drink. Then up comes old Willie Morris the mason, a man whose thirst was such the Mediterranean made of beer couldn't have quenched it, but a wonderful craftsman and he looks at the sundial and it wasn't sitting true. So he moves it and there's two half-crowns. . . . So he looks up to heaven and straight from the Bible says, in Welsh, "Oh God, thou has remembered thy children." Then later on old James comes out and he finds his money missing and he's going around the town saying, "This is the Devil's work. . . ." They couldn't both be right.

'All those old characters — all dead and gone! They don't make them like it any more. The modern world has killed them all, especially that thing [the television]. Nobody talks, nobody reads, nobody converses. You could listen to the men of the land talking about what they knew and they were happy men in many ways but they were not mindless machine minders. They lived by their crafts and they knew all about them.

'The craftsman wasn't considered. I remember a chap telling me in Lincolnshire about the people in his factory. He said a few years back they were getting 30s. a week hoeing swedes, now they're getting £30 a week but I'm still only getting £8 a week and I'm a tool setter and without my setting up the tools they couldn't work. They've got nothing but without me they couldn't do a stroke.

'The two great things in Wales were the secondary education and the religion. They wanted the secondary education here in Llandeilo and there was my uncle, a single man, living in this house with his sister and another old man came down from Cardigan, Shenkin Jones. He'd started as a tanner. The two old men were wealthy but tight and two ministers came to see them.

'One of these was old Dewi. A huge, black-faced, square man with a big beard — a great actor him — and I remember him in the chapel with the thumping of the Bible and the handkerchief blowing and the snorting and he'd shout and then drop his voice down down and say to the congregation, "Do you know what Hell is like? If the Tafy flowed into the Towy and the Towy into the Severn and the Severn flowed into the Thames and they all got together and flowed into the Rhone and the Rhine and they were joined by the Nile and the Amazon and the whole lot poured over the edge into Hell it would only be — phtt, that — on the surface of a smoothing iron. . . ."

'Well that was Dewi and he said to my uncle and Shenkin that they wanted the secondary education in Llandeilo. They had twenty-four students and the ministers of the town would give a year's teaching for nothing. They used some old pews to make into desks. Now even with all that you couldn't set up a school without a guarantee for a £1000. That was in the days you could build a damn good house for £300 — that £1000 was three houses. Those houses today sell for £25,000 so you can see what the kind of sum was they needed guaranteed. Now my uncle he sent for his cheque book and severally and together he and Shenkin signed a cheque for £1000 to be held as a guarantee. They gave Dewi the cheque and off he went. Now the power in the land was the magistrates and there was only one class that became magistrates and that was the landed gentry.

'It was kept for them. Now the main magistrate was Lord Emlyn, son of the Earl of Cawdor who owned all the valley. He was also Chairman of the Great Western Railway. If you said today he was President of General Motors it gave you some idea of his standing in the town. He owned half Scotland and most of South Wales.

'So he sees Dewi and says this secondary education is a very fine thought but he didn't want it. You see his cheap labour would have been gone. He thought the working classes were never meant to rise. So he said, "Now, you see, gentlemen, you can't have your school without a guarantee of £1000." And old Dewi pulls his trump card and booms out, "Here, my lord, is a cheque for £1000 from two gentlemen in Llandeilo − stop us now if you can!"

'Now the Emlyns have gone, the Cawdors have gone, the whole damn lot have gone − but so have we. The greatest export out of Wales today is ability. The secondary school was the foundation of Wales but it denuded Wales of its talent. It all went across into England. Only the mugs like me were left behind working on my craft. My son has gone, my daughter went.'

Mervyn told more stories to show how his family was linked back with Llandeilo's past.

'I have records of members of the family who were press ganged. One day some ships came to Carmarthen and offered free drink. Men flocked down there, down the hatches and they were given cupfuls of rum. When they came to it was dark and they were sick and there was a rolling motion and they'd been shanghaied and the captains took them out to Barbados and sold them to the sugar plantations. They had to wait until the Crimean war until they came back again to Carmarthen.

'Then there was a great, great uncle who'd been working at Taliaris, a good craftsman. Anyway he fell out with his old man and he picked up his tools and walked to Hereford and the press gang had taken a farmer's son. He was offering five gold sovereigns for anyone who'd go in his son's place so he took the money and went in his place and sailed with the fleet against the French. He was taken prisoner and then escaped.

'After he escaped he was in an engagement and he got a great cut on the head from a French cutlass and they rivetted a silver plate on his head. He was known as Will Pensioner. Every quarter he got £3 from the Government for his wound and he'd go on the booze and the head would swell against the plate and he'd not know what he was doing. He'd wake up miles away. When he was a very old man he lived at New Inn. My father remembers him as very old and blind and lighting his pipe with little metal tongs from the fire and he told my father about fighting against Napoleon. He lived until he was nearly 100, you see.

'Then back in 1770 there was the terrible murder of William Powell, Esquire − there was a book about it at the time. He was a beauty. He'd get his maids in the family way and kill them off and he'd an old plough and at night he'd pull it behind his horse and dump it on people's land and then charge them with theft and when their land was confiscated he'd buy it. So they all got together, including an ancestor of mine, and they waited in a little pub by the bridge called the Crown and they tooted up and blacked their faces and wore smocks and they killed old Powell.

'Now it went and snowed on the way back and they were caught by their footprints. They were tried in Hereford as feeling ran so high here in their favour against this bad lot, so they were found guilty there and hanged in Hereford. They were terrible men in those days. Some were cleverer thiefs than Powell − they applied the Enclosure Act. They just stole the land − they did just that! There's still a field in Fairfach called the Field of the Fair. It was all enclosed by Cawdor, the family just took it. It was the village green, actually.

'Now it's me who's old and there'll be none of my family working after me, there'll be no links. I wish I'd written it all down. When I was a little boy I met a man of 95 and he told me when he'd been a boy he'd gone to a funeral up the mountain and there had been a sin eater. They had brought out the coffin and passed the money and bread and salt and passed them to him over the coffin and he took upon him the sins of that man. Of course that goes back to the old religion.

'Now I feel like the old man when the minister asked him what he'd noticed most about life − it sounds better in Welsh, mind you − and, ah well, said the old boy, we're exactly like a wheel. It takes something to get it going, and then it gathers speed and now, Minister, by God, it's going like Hell. . . .'

Some years ago Mervyn Williams bought a little carving in a sale for 7s. 6d., because he thought the workmanship good. Later, he decided to sell it as he had been very ill and unable to work. It caused a good deal of mirth in the town when he said he was taking it to Sotheby's. It was valued, authenticated and sold and Mervyn had the last laugh. The carving was by Benvenuto Cellini.

2

The tinners

It is impossible to do more here than give a very brief introduction to the Cornish miner — for the student who wants to go into the subject in depth there are a number of excellent histories available — but some background is necessary to see the following accounts in perspective.

Cornish tin was traded from the very earliest times. We know that the Phoenicians came for tin and there are a host of legends stemming from those days, not the least that Jesus Christ came to Cornwall with Joseph of Arimathea who traded for tin.

Tin was streamed in the early days (and some tin streaming continued into the 1960s) but by the end of the sixteenth century miners had begun to burrow underground and some of their old workings can still be seen. But Cornish metals — copper, then tin — really came into their own in the eighteenth and nineteenth centuries and this was the heyday of the Cornish miner. The later discoveries of tin in Malaya and Australia dealt a blow to the Cornish mining industry from which it never recovered and our two accounts, by 'J.H.' and Raymond Harry, belong to the declining years of the industry.

But there is no doubt that even to this day it has marked the landscape. The mine 'castles', those granite engine houses, four square like Norman forts, scatter across the Cornish landscape from the north coast to the south and along the whole of the county's spine. Their crumbling chimney stacks are landmarks. It is difficult to imagine now when driving along peaceful roads and lanes, surrounded by these ruins, what it must have looked like when the furnaces were burning, the beam engines thumping and the stamps, the processing plants, were in full swing.

Whole families and large communities were dependent on mining. Some of the more fortunate families also had smallholdings — like 'J.H.'. Others did not. They died young. The average age of death of a miner on the 'tin coast', that is, the north coast of west Cornwall, was about 42. They were buried two and three deep in the churchyards. The mines were very wet and tuberculosis was rife. The age was even lower in some mines and at one point miners working in one of the oldest mines in the county, Ding Dong (between Penzance and Zennor) had finished their working lives through ill health before they were 30 years old.

Yet in many ways they were a hearty breed and they were, like the fishermen, very independent indeed. There were two methods used for employing labour. Contracting — where the mine owner paid the men to work for him on a day or piece work basis — and tributing. The latter carried a great deal more prestige.

Tributing was a form of sub-contracting. A group of men would band together and take on the mining of a section of a mine for which they received an agreed proportion of the value of the ore extracted. It was obviously in their own interests, therefore, to work as quickly, skilfully and economically as possible. There was always the chance too that the lode might prove better than was thought when the deal was concluded, thus making a higher profit for the tributers, although sometimes, of course, the reverse could happen.

If the lode did just peter out into what was called a 'horse' of barren ground, then the tributers were still left with their own expenses for candles, powder and smiths' charges. Tributers always took a gamble in that very often they would have to wait weeks to be paid, after their ore had been treated and assayed. Mine managers (known as captains) had to be up to all kinds of dodges from attempts to conceal promising lodes to changing the marks by which their rate of progress was measured. Stealing other tributers' ore was punished by hard labour and those who broke their contracts, giving up a pitch before the next 'setting day' (when the contracts were agreed) was punishable both by hard labour and by the miners having to give up the ore they had already extracted.

Son would follow father into tributing, as indeed families followed each other into contract mining (known in the early days as tutworking) and in this way a Cornish miner had an extremely careful apprenticeship. Very often an entire family would be employed, the youngsters of 9 and 10 wheeling barrows, the younger women employed in the processing sheds. 'J.H.' actually overlaps the days when women, 'bal maidens', were still employed in the Cornish tin mines.

The mining villages cling to the coast as indeed do the mines themselves, the stacks sometimes rising straight out of the cliff. There are still areas of the tin coast where little grows because of the pollution caused years ago from the arsenic which was part of the smelting process. Many of the little villages are dour terraces of small granite cottages in neat rows around the chapel. Even the lush valleys of the Fal and Helford rivers have the remains of old mines and some of the picturesque villages like Devoran quay would have been unrecognisable in the mid-nineteenth century. The decaying quay would have been alive with ships, a railway ran down from the mines at the head of the valley to a works at what is now called Point, and the river itself would have been thick and full of spoil from the mines. There was little trace of the holiday land so beloved of summer visitors.

Life was hard. I can remember, years ago, old ex-miners telling of walking to work at St Ives Consols — nearly 12 miles across the moors — and then back at the end of the shift and all for 10s. a week on contract. Overcrowding in the homes was a fact of life. Mother, father and perhaps ten children plus other relatives would share a two-bedroomed cottage, the beds being fitted around the shift system of the miners and kept almost continuously occupied. Disease in the mining towns like Camborne and Redruth was endemic.

Other miners' cottages straggled across moorland and it was these miners' families, like J.H.'s, who could rent a piece of land on which to grow vegetables and keep a pig and chickens.

In the eighteenth century a miner could acquire a piece of land and if he built his house on it within twenty-four hours in some cases, or between dawn and midnight in others, it was his. This meant getting the walls up as far as the roof and the hearth in, the roof could be turfed or thatched later.

One can only wonder at some of the work that went into the houses. I lived for years in what had been a miner's cottage and the open fireplace in one room was comprised of two huge granite slabs, about 5 foot high, by 2 foot wide and probably 5 or 6 foot across, on top of which went an enormous cross piece with a span of around 7 or 8 feet.

For recreation there were the various village feast days which usually ended in drunkeness and fighting (there was great inter-village rivalry) and chapel going. Like the fishermen, most mining families were very devout.

By the time Raymond Harry, who gives his account here, had left Levant Mine the great days of Cornish tin were over. There were still some tributers left on the tin coast but they were a dying breed. They had long since emigrated, sometimes to reappear later as old men after years in the Far East, the United States or Australia. There are very few people now left who can give a first-hand account of the old methods of working tin and copper.

James Hosking — mine engine driver

The diary of James Hosking came into the possession of Mrs Phyllis Pawlyn of Newlyn in Cornwall, from her uncle, William Thomas. The two men met when James (known as 'J.H.') was the engine driver at the old Boscaswell United Mine which closed in the early part of this century. When he was an old man he wrote down some of his memories, based on diaries he had kept when he was young, and he gave them to Mr Thomas who, in turn, left them to his niece.

The period covered is from 1871 to 1908 and it is neatly written into an old exercise book. Not only is it a remarkable first-hand account of days long ago in the tin mines, but it also provides a detailed description of life on a small hill farm, along with a vocabulary of phrases and words most of which have passed out of common usage in Cornwall – some from the old Cornish language, some dialect terms.

'Mining was the great industry. People worked hard, lived hard, loved offspring and had big families. Cornwall is the most healthiest place in the world. No one dies from it being too cold, no one dies from it being too hot. Cornish men quatty [creep] for no man, he stands in his own defence. We are found in almost every hole and corner of the world – North America, South America, Australia, New Caledonia and South Africa. The Cornish miner was in America long before Washington was President of the USA, and he had got as far as the Rocky Mountains before Washington was even born.

'Metalliferous mines are quite different from coal mines. The beds, or seams of coal, is horizontal in the ground and extend a long way through the ground. They do no boring to mine out the coal. The coal miner lays on his side, with pick or mattock, and hews out the coal. The metal miners are vertical chiefly, some mines incline more or less. The lode, vein or reef extends to a great depth in the ground. The miner begins at the surface to hulk, bore and shut. Hulk means cutting the lode that is against the hard granite. With hammer and peeker they cut sufficient to give the explosive a better chance to break the ground, and that is what the miners have to do – hulk, bore and shut. The word 'blast' was not much spoken by the old Cornish miner. When the miner starts to sink a shaft, they fix a windlass on the shaft to wind up the "stuff" or broken ground, and when they get deep and hard for manpower to wind up the stuff, they fix up a whipsederry to haul it.

'The whipsederry is a tackle fixed on the shaft with a pulley wheel on it and a horse employed to haul up the stuff. The rope is passed over the pulley wheel, then the horse hooked on to the end of the rope and it walks straight along until the kibble is up and they go on hoisting this way and that until at length the shaft gets to be deep and gets to be too hard work for the horse and as necessity is the mother of inventions, they build a horse whim to hoist the stuff. By the use of the horse whim they go on mining for many years.

'When I was at the age of 9 years, I was put to drive the two horses that worked the horse whim. The shaft was very deep

(240 fathoms) and all the ground mined out was hoisted with the horse whim. I can well remember, when there, driving the horses, garbed in corduroy knickers and a dicky made of duck and when it rained the material shrinks and keeps out lots of wet. The horses working in the whim go round and round, the whim cage or drum is overhead, the ropes are around the cage with each [going] to the kibbles — one kibble at the bottom of the shaft, the other kibble at the surface. The horses walking around pulled up the full kibble while at the same time the empty one goes down. It was only three or four months that I was driving the horses working the whim. A skip road was put in the shaft and the stuff was then hoisted to the surface by steam engine and that was the last of the horse whim at the mine.

'For four years after driving the horses in the whim, I was employed driving a horse hauling the stuff to the stamps [processing plant] and still wearing my dicky and knickers. The dicky is a short smock frock, generally worn by farm labourers.'

James went to work at Boscaswell Mine, near Pendeen, on the north coast of Cornwall in the heart of what used to be known as 'the tin coast'. Boscaswell, he says, was one of the oldest and deepest mines — 220 fathoms deep, with eight shafts, six in a row with one another. 'The mine was commonly known as Skale Downs, for short. "Skale" was spoken for Boscaswell. I seldom heard the full name spoken – in Boscaswell village they did say "down Skale".' James's uncles and grandfather worked in the mine. The mine produced both tin and copper and he reckoned it had certainly been worked well before the age of steam,

'or might have been in the days of King Arthur or at the time when the Phoenician merchants came from the East to Marazion (Marketjew) to buy tin. It may be some of the tin was from Scale . . . In olden times, mining operations was very slow and sparey. When resources and convenience was not available as in those days there was no steel, the boyers and miners' tools soon got blunt and bralled. The drills for boring the holes was called "Boyers". There was no carts nor any wheel conveyance to haul the ore raised from the mine to the stamps, donkeys and mules were employed to carry the tin stuff on their backs, the ore was put in sacks and loaded on the donkey's back and work was carried on as circumstances permitted.

'Miners have a special signal to call for help, if at any time it is needed. If a miner is working by himself and his light goes out, and he be in the dark or wanted any help, he takes the hammer and taps or beats against the solid ground similar to the following:

♩♩	♪♪♪	♪♩	♪♪♩	♪♪♩	♩♩	♪♪♪	♪♩	♪♩	♪♪♩	etc.
1 1	1 2 3	1 2	1 2 3	1 2 3	1 1	1 2 3	1 2	1 2	1 2 3	

Other miners, hearing the sound, will rush to his assistance. Cornish miners working together call each other "comrade". It is all comrade this and comrade that. The time working in the mine, they call it "coore", shift was not mentioned − "forenoon coore", "afternoon coore" and "night coore." "What coore ar'ee?" "I'm afnoon coore to bal this week." The miners' lunch they do take with them underground is chiefly bread and butter, they seldom take anything that is heavy to eat in the mine, such as currant friggen, figgy-fuggen, apple dicky or toad-in-the-hole. Fuggens is unleavened bread − flour, lard or suet, a pinch of salt, currants or raisins, all put in the flour and mixed into pastry. Apple dicky is apples cut in small pieces and mixed with the flour same as currents and raisins. The fuggen is oblong, about one inch in thickness and the size for a feed at one time. Toad-in-the-hole is about the same as fuggen but they cut a hole in the pastry and put a bit of beef in it. I have eaten some squall of them in my day. "Squall" was a term for a great number at a time.

'The miners' lunch is "mossle" . . . it is carried in a small bag made for the purpose called a "mossle bag". The water for drinking they take in a sort of little barrel made of wood, carrying about 3 or 4 quarts. The little flat barrel is called a canteen and is carried like a knapsack.

'In all Cornish mines, measurements is reckoned by the fathom [six feet]. The miners working contract get so much per fathom for breaking or mining out the ground, all the ore, rock and ground miners break is called "stuff". When the stuff is hauled to the surface it is spalled, i.e. broke small and suitable for the stamps, where all the granite stone is picked out and wheeled over the burrow [waste dump].'

When a mine closed it was called 'knocking the bal'. Skale Downs, according to James, had been idle for twenty years and 'knocked' until 1858 when it was restarted by a manager, Captain Will Noy (all mine managers were called captains). He got up a company of Penzance financiers who formed a private company and Captain Noy then commenced 'to fork out the water' (drain the mine), and also mined the old dumps for any residues of tin left from earlier days. Those who put up the money for the mine were called **adventurers** and Skale must have done well as within a comparatively short time Captain Noy had made enough money to pay back the adventurers the money they had invested, plus a dividend, after having paid all the expenses. The bal was again 'knocked' in 1874 'due to the Drunkeness of the Directors and bad management'. During the sixteen years the mine was worked for the last time there was not a fatal accident nor loss of sight or limb.

'When I was at the age of 18 years I went to work underground to fill the skip in Skale Downs, which afforded me a good chance of seeing what it was like underground. At the time four shafts were in use. The pumping engine shaft and three others were used for hauling or hoisting the stuff. The shafts were a long way from each other and the ladder way was in the engine shaft, 220 fathoms deep.

'The miners go by ladder way to and from their work. In going through the levels and from shaft to shaft, I have seen what all the mine is like.'

Skale, says James, was a healthy mine as tin mines went. It had good ventilation and was safe as the ground was hard and firm. 'In some places the side walls were smooth as a glass bottle.' It was not perpendicular, but inclined to 70 or 75 degrees.

'Two men were employed filling the skip, the lander at the surface then emptied the skip. When leavework time came, the lander tied a string round a small stick of timber and tied it to the bow of the skip, which is called a "dickey". When we saw the dickey come, we'd quickly drop our shovels in the skip and away through the level to the ladder and then climb to the surface.

'I did not like working underground. In preference I took to engine driving of the hauling engine as they called the stone whim. There were three engines in the mine, the pumping engine, an engine to work the stamps and the hauling engine. They were the Cornish beam engines. There was never any other machinery in use on the mine, never an air compressor or boring machine, neither a stone breaker on the mine. Everything was done by hand labour underground and at surface.

'The tin dressing was done by hand labour.' [This was largely done by women who were known as 'bal maidens.'] 'The old people managed to get through with their work and were happy and comfortable. When driving the engine on night shift, the driver worked by the light of a tallow candle. There was no paraffin oil nor lamps in those days. Outside working candles were carried by a horn lantern.'

He gives the names for different pieces of mining tackle and various processes. The beam of the Cornish engine was called a 'bob'. The headgear on a shaft was called 'popedheads'. The 'spalling floors' were where the stuff, when hauled from underground, was dumped. The men spalled it to a suitable size for the stamps and picked out all the granite and stone. Stuff hauled from underground without ore in it was called 'deads'. There was little labour involved in dressing copper ore.

'The men spall or break the big lumps of copper ore, pick out and throw away the waste and then the women do the bucking of copper. They stand at their work with a flat hammer and reduce the copper to the size of rough gravel. The copper is then ready for market.

'The stamps hollars is where the tin is dressed and where

they work under a shelter or roof with the front all open. In cleaning and dressing the tin quite a number of hands are employed, mostly young women and boys. There is much labour in cleaning the tin, buddling, trunking, toasing and framing. The women chiefly do the framing, working under shelter but facing the open air. Toasing is the last stage of cleaning tin. Keeves are used for toasing. A keeve is a big tub about 3½ feet high and about 3½ feet in diameter. It is half filled with water and a man with a shovel stirs the water whilst another man shovels in the work until the keeve is full. When a keeve is full a big block of timber is used to pack the keeve as quick as they can do it and the tin settles to the bottom. When it is settled hard, they drain off the water with a siphon, then skim off 2 or 3 inches off the top of the toasing. The tin in the keeve is then fit for market. Everything in Skale Downs was done in the same way as hundreds of years ago.'

The Cornish mining families tended to have the same surnames so they acquired nicknames. One family of Williams were nicknamed 'Boagers' 'they were wonderful musicians, bandsmen and bandmasters; another family Williams was nicknamed Cobbler.' Yet another Williams family was nicknamed 'Gooner and they were good singers and good for step dancing.'

James's list of nicknames sounds like something out of Henry Fielding or late seventeenth-century Restoration comedies — Will Tearem, John Gogleye, Jim Dinion, Tom Pilchard, Tom Duck, Steve Moonlight, Tom Satan. 'I knew a man nicknamed "skiddamalank", a healthy, strong, well able man, he was very lazy and was put out to prison to tread the wheel. He had to pump or drown.' Two particular tearaways were twin brothers, Bob and Jan, known locally as the 'Morvah Devils'.

'My mother was brought up on a little farm in Morvah. I have heard her speak of one harvest time when her people was on the point of going to harvest a field of wheat and before they had a chance to do so, during one night Bob and Jan had been there, cut the field of wheat, bound it, took the sheaves of corn over in an adjoining field and made it up in round aris mows, all complete. The great mystery was how it could be possible that two chaps could do such a trick in one night as the field is more than an acre of ground.'

Times grew hard in mining and, according to James, both Jan and Bob went to sea but in different ships. Years later two captains met in the bar of a hotel in the Far East and one told the other he had a man who 'will fight any man you've got on your ship'. The challenge was accepted and agreed on. The two men were brought on to one of the ships, looked at each other and just stared. There was no fight. It was Bob and Jan.

James came from smallholding stock, one of the little hill farms rather like a Scottish croft. Few can now recollect what it was like to live that kind of life. Farming had, of course, no subsidies then. The soil is thin and the landscape very windswept but miners who did have land to utilise as well as their work were very fortunate.

As in Ireland, the west coast of Scotland and other similar terrains, the fuel burned on the old Cornish ranges was either furze or peat. Furze was old bracken and gorse. A man cut the furze with a heavy reap hook in one hand and a 'cuff' (a leather glove) on the other and he would cut a 'task'. 'A task', says James, 'is just what a man can hold in his hands placing it on the ground.' In the season, when furze was plentiful, men and women were employed. The men made up the bundles which were called trusses. 'The women did lead the horses, which was loaded with two trusses, one on each side. They did lead the horses home then while the men continued to cut furze and then they would jump on the horse's back and gallop back for another turn.' James says that the women were regularly employed in this way and that 'it was a time of more fun than work. I have heard my mother speak of it and the fun she had bringing home the furze and the turf [peat] too, also in its season.'

Pride of place in Cornish kitchens went to the old, cast-iron kitchen ranges, something like a very primitive Aga or Rayburn today. They were called 'slabs' even in my days — presumably a throwback to the way things used to be cooked when James Hosking was a boy. 'In my early days', he says, 'there was no slabs used in many places, no such cooking ranges. Everything was done in the open chimney. In the chimney was kept two baking irons. The baking iron was a round flat iron with a handle to it. One iron was about 20 inches or 2 feet in diameter, another about 14 to 16 inches, each iron about half an inch thick.' The woman baked on these flat, slab-like surfaces. 'There was also a "brandis", a piece of triangular iron with a leg corner. A turf was put each side and the kettle or pot boiled on it.'

To bake bread, the iron would be cleaned and put on a bed of hot ashes. A pot would be inverted over the bread, then that would be packed around with furze and turf and it would cook with little or no attention. 'In about one hour or so the bread was ready and baked beautiful, good enough for a king.'

A good deal of time had to be spent collecting fuel for the winter months, not only turf and furze but 'glaws', that is, dung which, when dried, made a good, hot fire.

'The women, when gathering fuel, often carried a sack to put it in and brought it home on their heads. Others used their "tousers" to carry it up. The touser is a big apron made of sacking with four strings to tie it, two long ones to tie around the waist and two short to tie behind, lower down. They would fill up the touser and tie up the four corners and also carry that on their heads.

'Many miners would agree with a farmer for a splat of ground in which to till potatoes. The splat would be from 10 to 15 laces — a lace is 18 feet square on 36 feet long and 9 feet wide. The farmer kept a measuring stick 9 feet long he called a gourd. The splat of ground was measured with the gourd, 4 gourds long and one gourd wide was a lace. The price charged per lace in my young day was 1s. A miner tilling 15 laces would have a good crop of potatoes, enough to serve through the winter and often had sufficient to keep a pig too. With potatoes and flour, the miner would feed the pig until fat enough to kill and after it was killed it was made into ham, bacon and some of it salted into the bussa. The bussa was an earthenware pot in which salted meat or fish was kept.'

The miners also ate the salt fish mentioned before, calling it niflin.

'I have often made a good meal of boiled niflin and potatoes cooked in their skin with a drop of dippy on the plate too. Dippy is a thin cream. Pilchards from the coast villages also provided good fare. Croust is the food you eat between meals at harvest time but I never remember harvest without croust from start to finish. Yet when harvest is finished, I heard nothing more of croust. No matter how many were working in the fields, croust was brought out to all hands, men, women and children. It came about ten o'clock in the morning and again about four in the afternoon — bread and butter, cake, and a kettle of tea with plenty of milk and sugar.'

The harvest of James Hosking's day bears little resemblance to today's heavily automated activity. There was little storage room for the corn or hay.

'The seal is the foundation for the ricks of corn or hay and its purpose is to keep the ricks up from the damp ground. It is about 8 or 9 inches high, made of small stones, so that water may percolate and keep the bottom of the rick dry. The space between seals is called an ally and is kept clear so that no water shall lodge around the ricks. The mowhay is the yard where ricks of corn and hay is kept, the bigger the farm, the bigger the mowhay.

'Now the Guldize is the great day of bringing in the last of the corn when the harvest is finished. There was no waggon and the corn was carried on horses' backs. Farmers did help each other, here today, there tomorrow, some other place next day. It was a busy time for men and women. The men worked in the fields making the sheaves into bundles and then tying them on to the backs of the horses. The women did lead the horses with the corn to the mowhay to the men building the rick there. Then the women would get on the horses and ride back for more and so they kept on carrying and bringing in the corn, like a constant stream, like a river. My mother did lead a horse when bringing in both corn and fuel — she was a good rider on horseback.

'At dinner we would have a big piece of beef in a crock, plenty of potatoes and vegetables and a figgy pudding. Figgy pudding is pastry not made dry but made with plenty of beef suet and raisins.'

Although the work was hard James says

'the people who lived in my granny's time and my mother's time were far more happy than people living in the present time. I can well remember both my two grannies and I can remember one when she was 70 walking from Camborne to St Just and carrying with her an American clock.' (That is a distance of well over 20 miles.)

There were no thrashing machines able to get to small hill farms even when they had come into general use in the west country so it was all done by hand with a flail called a thrashel. 'The corn in the barn was thrashed and the straw used for bedding for cattle and pigs. The reed which was left over was sold, sometimes for thatch. To thrash 100 sheaves was one man's day's work.'

The old people, remembers James, had some quaint sayings. To be busy at work was 'ripping to'n like Betty Kemp in the brambles' or 'tearing to'n like a bull in a turfy hedge or a dog digging for daylight'. When feeling cold they would be 'scriffed up like a Peewit or gathered up like John-she-wal'. A howling baby 'screeched like a witrick' and an old man was 'grizzled like a badger'.

Perhaps we should end with one of his earliest memories. Cornish villages then as, indeed, now, were very proud indeed of their silver bands, known further north as brass bands. Villages competed against each other and bandsmen wore smart uniforms covered with braid and they were the envy of small boys. Now the Morvah band had 'a great brass instrument, what it was I did not know but it was pronounced such as Upperklite or Orphocledie or some such I think. I had a feeling of tremendous ambition to have this great instrument and to play in such a band. I asked Mother to buy it me and at length she consented saying "ess [yes] James, my son, when money do grow on ferns you shall have a music." At that I was much pacified.'

Raymond Harry

I first met Raymond Harry in the early 1960s. He had returned
to live in Cornwall, in his later years, after a long time abroad,
and he was always at the centre of some storm over the
opening up of tin mines in places which had seen no mining
for years and become local beauty spots. He was a spare man,
forthright to his critics, and he did not suffer fools gladly.

He was born in 1903 and his time in the Cornish tin mines
just overlapped with that of 'J.H.' but his story is different —
ending dramatically with the disaster at the Levant mine in
1919 and his subsequent self-imposed exile in mines in other
parts of the world. Unlike 'J.H.' he did not come from a small
farming background but from a mining family. His father had
also gone abroad to work — in South Africa — when jobs were
short and many of the Cornish mines no longer working. His
wife and family fended for themselves as best they could in a
tiny cottage on the coast.

Later Raymond Harry wrote down some of his early
memories, and especially about his time at Levant mine, for
the *Cornish Magazine* under the pen name 'Jack Penhale'.
Unlike 'J.H.' he was a true underground miner and it is this
side of his life in the mines I have used from his account to
show a different aspect to that of 'J.H.'

Levant is known as 'the mine under the sea'. Following the
great disaster of 1919, which Raymond Harry describes in
graphic detail, it remained closed until the late 1970s. It is now
working again for the first time for fifty years as part of the
Geevor mine complex at Pendeen. It clings to the cliff edge on
the north coast, that same tin coast remembered by 'J.H.' from
his days in the long defunct Scale mine. It is about 4 miles
south of it.

Raymond Harry remembers.

'Levant stretched a mile and a half or so under the sea. I've
worked there in temperatures of 120 degrees when it was as
hot as hell, listening to the boulders crash on the sea bed above
my head.

'My father died of the dust at only 43, leaving a widow and
seven children. I had to go down the mine to keep them.'

Before starting work on his first day his mother gave him the brass waterproof matchbox which had belonged to his father. On his arrival at Levant older miners showed him how to 'take a handful of wet clay, shape it into a holder and stick it on my helmet with about an inch and a half or so protruding' and they then set off to ride the man engine down to the depths some 2000 feet below.

As it was the man engine which was to cause the disaster it is worth hearing Harry's description of it as it was a method used throughout the tin mines for the miners to get down to the various levels, the alternative being climbing up and down by ladders. When ladders had to be used the men could spend anything from one to two hours just getting to their place of work.

First he had to stand on a small platform next to the giant plunging rod.

'The huge wooden rod which descends into the shaft is just 1600 feet from top to bottom and there are small platforms of steps attached to it all the way down at 12-foot intervals. At the sides of the shaft there are corresponding platforms, also spaced at 12-foot intervals. These platforms were called sollars.'

On his first day another miner joined Harry on the platform to show him what to do.

'As the step rose I was told it's here, step on it. I had to hold on to an iron handle attached to the rod about 4 feet above every step. As the beam reached the bottom of its stroke we stepped off on to the sollar and then up comes another step and we step on to that.'

It needed a nice sense of timing, stepping off and on in time to the beat of the beam, the light diminishing as they travelled downwards until it was pitch dark

'and we could only tell where we were by the feel of the handle. You can feel the rod hesitate before it goes down again and it was in that second as the beat changed that the miners got off and on. There were 133 steps on the beam so that 133 men were on it at any one time. It took half an hour for the first man to get to the bottom but after that six men would arrive every minute.

'It was quite quiet that engine, it made no noise at all. At the different levels you could feel the draughts from the launders.' Launders were the drains which took the water out of the mine through adits (passageways) into the sea. 'At one level, sixty fathoms, it was like a church and you could hear the sound of the men singing.

'Then you pass sea level and still keep on going down. On the first day my neck was stiff and aching from keeping the candle upright in my helmet but you get used to that, of course, quite quickly. We kept going down — on, down, off; on, down, off, we pass 150-fathom level where there is hardly room to stand, down to the 170-fathom level and finally leave the road at the 266-fathom level.'

This journey was to be repeated every day that Harry worked in the mine.

Nor was this the end of the descent for then the miners in the bottom level had to use iron ladders to reach that — 278 fathoms below the surface for Harry, 302 for some of the others.

'It was fairly well lit down there by about a dozen candles and there was a small railway going in to the tunnel. Then came a rattling and rushing kind of a noise and the skip arrived in which the ore was hoisted to the surface.

'We were taught everything by the old miners, even the burning of candles was something of an art. The men paid by the day were issued with a packet of candles on a Monday morning. A packet weighed 3 lbs and consisted of thirty-six candles.

'Miners would try and save a few candles if they could which they would then sell to local shopkeepers. It would give him a shilling or two for beer and made a bigger profit for the shop.'

At the time Harry worked at Levant, a full man's wage was

about £4 a month. Not surprisingly any money that could be made on top of that was very welcome indeed. It was a long working day for a boy of 13 which started at 5.30 a.m. when his mother woke him up to go to work, and which began in the dark, was spent in the dark, and very often ended in the dark by the time the miners had ridden the beam up to the surface.

The boys were made to do all kinds of different jobs and Harry spent some time with the mine blacksmith who was responsible for looking after all the iron work underground. He was also responsible for seeing that the pumping engine was kept in good order. The pumping engine was similar to the man engine but, as its name suggests, it was used for pumping the water out of the mine — virtually all Cornish mines were very wet and constant pumping was required to make them workable.

Along the sides of the shaft that housed the engine were ladders used for maintenance purposes and one day water began pouring back down the shaft. Harry and the blacksmith had to climb the ladders to discover where the leak was.

'The water came down in torrents, it poured down on us. We just had to keep climbing. We reached the 266-fathom level and it still came. Climbing a shaft like that was bad enough in good conditions but with the water it was a hundred times worse. We had to keep on feeling for the ladders in the dark and wet and climbing ever up and up and up and still the water came.

'Only those who worked in that mine can imagine such ladders and such sollars as there were in that shaft and the timbers used at this time. Rungs that should have been half an inch of steel were only about an eighth of an inch thick, rungs that should have been straight were bent. In one or two places there were no staves at all. Where there should have been good, stout sollars, the planking was slippery and dangerous and where there should have been protection from the plunging beam, there was none at all.

'We climbed 600 feet in those conditions, foot by foot. At the top of some of the ladders we had to step right, at the others, left and yet again we would find the bottom of the ladder behind that we'd just climbed. Above and below was hundreds of feet of nothing and the water still coming. When you felt all the weight on your arms and hands you knew you were on the overhanging part of the ladder.'

They reached the 70-fathom level before finding the source of the leak.

This was a broken pipe 'so corroded inside that the water could not get through and what should have been a 9-inch hole was only 3 inches and the water pressure had burst the pipe'. After making a temporary repair, Harry and the blacksmith climbed again until they reached one of the adits — where the launders take the water out to the sea — and found themselves in sunshine looking down at the sea below. They had 'walked' from the 278-fathom to the 40-fathom level, by ladder, without light.

Harry was a 'contract miner', not a tributer, and contract miners kept to the main lodes of tin as they were not paid to bother with any side shoots, however promising these might look. However they would pass on information they thought might be useful to their tributing friends and if the tributers did well out of the information they would usually pass on a bonus to the contract worker who had told them.

Only once did Harry know of the sea breaking into Levant and then 'a barge loaded with cement was towed to the spot and the whole cargo dumped over the hole to seal it off.'

It was some time before Harry was allowed to be present at blasting, when explosives were used to loosen the ore-bearing rock. Down at the 326-fathom level, there was some compressed air used for ventilation but in spite of this it was known as Little Hell. 'The first time I saw a miner unlace his boots and put his foot in the air I thought it was water that ran out — later I knew it to be sweat.' The miners at the bottom levels would clamber over the rocks and rubble of previous workings, climbing over piles of broken ore sometimes twenty feet high.

All the boys had learned to use 'hammer and drill' to make holes in the rock for all sorts of purposes but the most difficult was to be able to do this upwards.

'The dust which comes down keeps trickling on to your

chest and body and mixes with sweat until you are covered in grey dust. You kept hammering at the drill, then turning it just a little bit, then hammering it again to chip the bottom of the hole in a different place with the next hammer blow. All through the mine you could hear the tap, tap, some in the same "end" doing the same thing, others below busy hammering away, others up above thumping at the drills, boring the holes.

'Then a miner prepares the dynamite and fuses for blasting. He took about fifteen sticks of the stuff and cut five pieces of fuse about 2½ feet long to begin with and then each length about 2 inches longer than the one before to allow the holes to be blasted in rotation.

'Then he would get out the detonators from a little box and then came a really stupid, ignorant and evil piece of practice. Instead of using the special pincers provided to tighten the detonator on to the fuse, he would put the cap in his mouth and bite it until it was secure.

'One false bite and the whole lot would have exploded but they all did it and I never heard of anyone meeting sudden death by doing so. I did it myself in the end. Then the dynamite is packed into the holes and a primer pushed in on top. Some fine earth was wrapped in paper and put in above the primer and tamped tight with a wooden stick called a charger. The fuse was left dangling. When all the holes are filled, all the belongings were taken up, the canteen emptied, and the miners went, leaving one behind to fire the holes. He fires his holes rushes down the to the next man who then fires his and so on down a line and then all the miners wait in comparative safety for the noise of the explosions, counting them to make sure all the sticks have gone off.'

On October 20 1919 it was all to change.

'For some time there seemed to have been a little tremble on the beam engine when the men were riding it and several of the older men had said that it was not running as smoothly as it should be. Nobody took much heed of what they said but some were so worried they actually left the mine all together. So there was no question that there had been warnings.

'However for most of us youngsters it seemed all right. We hadn't enough experience of it to know there might be something wrong.' As the day shift finished the men rushed to get on the engine. Harry had climbed up part of the way on ladders and caught the beam engine on the 190-fathom level.

'It was the custom for some of the younger men to climb part of the way by ladder and ride the engine nearer the surface to relieve the congestion down below and give the older miners a chance to ride all the way up. I got off as usual at the top, followed by one other miner, and went into the changing room.

'After a few minutes I realised that nobody else had appeared and we all went back to see what was happening. Then a miner came rushing back up the passageway shouting, "the engine is gone, the engine is gone". The rhythmic noise of the engine had stopped and instead came a noise I can only describe like all the souls screaming in Hell. The main pin which had held the great beam had worn through and the beam had plummeted down, full of men standing on its steps and shearing off the sollars at the side of the shaft on its way. Thirty-one men died immediately and nearly a hundred more were severely injured. One man was left standing on a piece of wood a foot square for three days before he was brought up and the dead could not be fully accounted for for nearly three weeks.'

The mine was closed and the row over responsibility was never resolved. A disaster fund was set up, partly financed by miners overseas, and it was still remembered with bitterness at the time of the Penlee lifeboat disaster in December 1981. There was still £30,000 in the fund at that time. Little of the money collected actually reached the dependants and one family could remember graphically how their mother had to plead with those who administered the fund for money to buy her fatherless children shoes. It was handed out as if it was workhouse charity.

There is one footnote to Raymond Harry's story of his escape from the disaster. After leaving Levant he worked in many other countries as a miner, beginning in Western Canada – he was one of the first men in the Porcupine mining camp. He worked in South Africa and Australia. He often wondered about the man who had come off the beam engine immediately behind him that fateful day, the very last man off the engine.

Forty years later, in the United States, he met a Cornishman who had read some of his anecdotes in the *Cornish Magazine.* 'So you're Raymond Harry,' he said. 'I must tell you. I read your book and I've been looking for you ever since. I had to find you to let you know I was the man behind you on the engine the day it broke. . . .'

In his latter years, Raymond Harry came back to Cornwall and was sad at the lack of tradition left there: 'all my generation is scattered throughout the Commonwealth.'

Mining never left his blood and he spoke of the romance of the old days.

'Even a little village like Zennor had 3,000 inhabitants and a mine with fourteen tin lodes. Wheal Vor which now supplies Helston with its water supply was the richest tin mine in the world in its day, producing 220 tons a month. There was even a mine at Wherrytown on Penzance beach which could only be worked for two hours at a time at low water. Yet if you tried to open up the old mines you could canvas every businessman up and down Market Jew Street in Penzance and only one or two would invest in opening a mine locally although some people will spend money on holdings in Australia and South Africa.'

Since he spoke to me a handful of mines have opened in a small way, Wellington and Wheal Jane near Truro and, indeed, Levant itself as part of the extended workings of Geevor mine, the only mine which remained in continuous production. Yet that kept going by drawing heavily on Italian and Polish labour, not the indigenous Cornish population.

'Too many Cornish mining families emigrated you see. Yet there's more tin in Cornwall than ever came out. But you know what they say about Amundsen? He wasn't the first man at the South Pole. When he got there he found a Cornishman sinking a shaft. . . .'

3

Dying for coal

My rose was cropped just in the bloom
My rising sun went down at noon,
In health and strength put not your trust,
The strength of living is but dust.
Dear friends go home and shed no tear,
I must lie here 'til Christ appear,
And when he comes I hope to have
A joyful rising from the grave.

This is the epitaph of one of the thirty-two miners who died in
a pit disaster at the Baxterley (now Baddesley) colliery in North
Warwickshire in May 1882. Before looking at that accident in
some detail — as it is referred to in the accounts which follow
— there are a number of points of interest which arose out of
talking to old miners.

While fishermen, oyster dredgers and, indeed, even tin
miners could talk nostalgically of the good old days I could not
find even one survivor from the days of the privately owned
mines who had a good word to say for the previous system.
They were prepared to say, as were others, elsewhere, that
people were more friendly in the old days, that although the
life outside work was hard, it had its compensations and that
much of it was good. But nobody thought that nationalisation

had done anything but improve working conditions and wages and most of them considered it to be an absolute blessing.

Both the miners whose memories follow this account of the disaster worked at Baxterley colliery and both suffered from coal-induced diseases. Both have died since giving the interviews, David Smalley in April 1982. The Baxterley pit belonged, before nationalisation, to the Dugdale family.

The Dugdale's mock Gothic castle still dominates the valley in which the pits are situated and the Dugdale family still lives there. There are many local memorials to the pit owner at the time of the disaster — William Stratford Dugdale, who also died in it. He went down into the mine as part of the first rescue mission and was injured during the first major explosion.

The main market town in the area is Atherstone, sliced in half by the A5, the Roman Watling Street, a major trunk route from London to Holyhead since Roman times. Most people when they think of Warwickshire picture in their minds Shakespeare's county — the south and west sides of Warwickshire, with its lush fields, woodlands, copses and willows along the banks of the lazily winding Avon. The countryside is still fertile in North Warwickshire — some of the most valuable farming land in the country — but underneath is the North Warwickshire coal field. It is still very active and produces a very high grade of coal.

Coal mining in the area goes back for centuries, traces of old workings remaining in the woods above today's mines.

The group of mines of which Baxterley was one was known as the Stratford mines. The chain of disaster began on the evening of Sunday 30 April when hot ashes from a pumping engine in a deep seam at the colliery set fire to some slack and coal. The fire was put out by men working nearby who thought no more about the incident.

At about six o'clock in the evening of 1 May 1882, eight men and a boy went down into the mine to go on evening shift at a distance of about a mile from the shaft bottom. Some three hours after they had entered the mine, a fire broke out half way between their place of work and the shaft bottom. Apparently it had started in the pumping engine installed in the return airway and travelled to the main intake airway through some opening.

News of the fire reached the pithead and a group of miners volunteered to go down to see if anything could be done to reach the unfortunate men in the workings. The next shift of men were working 1500 yards from the foot of the main shaft and as the fire again started to spread, they were completely cut off from escape at a depth of about 900 feet. While the rescue party were trying to damp down the flames, at about nine o'clock, there was a tremendous explosion. Rescue attempts went on during that day and the whole of the next while the fires still raged. Many of those rescued died later due to severe burns and during this period of time William Stratford Dugdale was badly injured, dying some days later.

The newspapers were full of first-hand accounts of the time but the Sanders family of Baxterley kept the diary written by William Sanders who was down the pit soon after the fire started.

The first the men knew was when smoke began to travel towards them.

'There were thurls or roads driven across from the incline into the return airway at certain distances and doors in them so that any foul air should be kept in return to the upcast shaft and straight to the fan. But somehow no one ever said that in one of these thurls, the door was opened and then smoke came down full force into the incline, the air taking it down until all the deep was filled with suffocating smoke. The men who had been working on Sunday night were all down there and were suffocated while a horse they had with them managed to get through to the stables and one man tried hard to get out as he was found afterwards on his hands and knees a way up the incline trying to get out. That was Joseph Horton whose father was cut off next morning. There were eight men and one lad and it was while trying to rescue these that the explosions occurred on 2 May 1882.

'Early on Tuesday morning May 2nd there came a woman knocking at our door and crying, "do you know the pit's on fire?" I was at home. We was playing short of sale (short time) or there might have been more there. I said I did not as it was always supposed to be safe. She said "it's on fire" and told me brother Joe is down. So I soon had my clothes on and off to the

pit. When I reached the Bank, there were a crowd of men and
women too weeping. They had been working hours then,
trying to get down the Deep and had to keep falling back.

'I was told they was using cloth. Now I had worked at a fire
before at Cockspur old pit under George Morgan, Manager,
and I thought I could help as miners as a rule are ever ready to
risk even life for a comrade so I said to W. Hough let's go and
help and we went down until we reached where they were at
work, using the cloth, when all at once I was filled with
dismay. Instead of using the cloth dividing the arch carrying
smoke away into return, keeping fresh air on the one side and
putting cloth up as you go on − when you may travel as fast as
the cloth can be put up (cloth acting as a chimney carrying
smoke or foul air away) − instead of that being the case they
had the cloth all across the arch trying to force the smoke back
where it came from. A thing impossible to do and every time
the cage went up and down the shaft it caused a greater rush,
so that those that were carrying or holding the cloth were
overcome and fell back.

'Then Mr Smallman who had come to help ordered the cloth
to be nailed up cross the arch and he asked me if I would help
a young man named Roland Till to do it. So this young man
went up a ladder to nail a cloth and I went with him but we
had hardly stepped off the ladder when the wind it roared and
the smoke it poured over the top of the cloth. A roar like
thunder, then came the fire as quick as lightning. I could not
describe it in any other way. A terrible thunder, then fire, so
that they who were on the bank never expected any to be left
alive. Then a cry, "run for your lives!" Just to think what it
would be like trying to run!

'I was enveloped in flame. I can remember trying to cover
my face with my hands at the same time fire burning around
my ankles and running up my trouser legs, blistering my
thighs, leaving its mark. Then as soon as the fire was spent
there was that deadly poison to breathe. Every breath we took
like boiling tar, scalding and burning the throat going down
into the lungs. I went as far as I felt able until I dropped on my
hands and knees with face near the ground then I could breathe
a little better. Talk about cries and tears − that was the time
many prayed that morning who had not for some good while.

'I kept on my hands and knees, creeping along. I got up the incline and instead of keeping on straight for the bottom of the pit, I made a turn and kept going until I bumped my head against a door. I knew then I was wrong so I sat down and thought come you must try to get back, no one will think of coming this way to search, so I made another try and crept. It seemed to be such a long way I thought I must have gone too far and was going to the stable and had gone by the way to the shaft, so I turned again, still on my hands and knees. I then found I bumped my head on the same door again and lay down and thought I must give in.

'Then the thought came to me that while there is life there is hope, try again asking the Lord to help, so starting again I kept on feeling and listening for the wire that was still running till I heard it, then feeling for the Bobbin Rollers as I found the wire running down, until it ran to the bottom. I have wondered many a time since that my hands were not cut off by those rollers.

'The air had got a bit cleaner then so I rose to my feet and called out, "is there anyone here that cannot get to the bottom?" No one spoke so I made my way to the bottom of the shaft as well as I could until I reached it and saw a ray of daylight just round the bottom and in that circle someone standing. So I said, "can we go up?" not knowing who it was and he said, "no we cannot. You must sit down in that manhole." I knew his voice and could tell it was Mr Pogmore (the mine Agent) so I said, "it's no use sitting down, sir, we must try and get up and he says, "we cannot. There has been an explosion and it has blown the bottom of the cage. We cannot get up." I made answer that I had had my share. The flesh of my hands hung in shreds, head and face charred, legs burnt even to thighs blistered. So I walked passed him and shouted up shaft as well as I could. "Can we come up and quickly?" and came the answer, "yes, get on." Looking, I saw the cage was settled in bottom right for getting on so walking to the cage I said to Mr Pogmore, "come on sir!" and he said, "how can I hold on to you." I said I would hold him if he would come to me and clasping the upright of the cage in the elbow of my right arm and putting my left arm around him, shouted, "go on!" and we were soon at the top and I shall never forget the words Mrs Pogmore said as she saw I was on the cage. She was watching and waiting and said, "thank the Lord he has come at last." They took him out of my arms and led him into the engine house and I never saw him again.'

Sanders then collapsed. He refused brandy, asking for oil which they fetched to drench his head and hands, 'then I took castor oil, sweet oil and when being dressed with neetsfoot oil in my throat which was scalded with the poisonous gas I had sucked down. This gas, fatal to many, was broken up by the oil.'

Four doctors gave him up and 'every morning the neighbours would look to see if the blinds were down. I was so near it I just breathed as it were to my throat.' His injuries were made worse by what he describes as 'brain fever'. It was six months before he could even dress himself: 'I had no hands I could use. They had been stripped of flesh and the nails all come off.'

A letter from another eye witness, Fred Marsh, says how the first rescue party, thirty-six strong, set off underground when a 'terrific explosion of gas occurred some distance away but the flames completely filled the road and there was nothing to see but one dense mass of flames. All were horribly scorched and burned.' Fred Marsh had volunteered for the second rescue party

'when another mass of gas exploded and filled everywhere with flame but by stuffing our caps into our mouths we managed not to breathe any of it, and burying our faces in the coat sleeves were not burned except for a little hair. So we made another attempt and got out thirty-three men, all alive but terribly burnt, nearly all had their eyes burnt quite out and their tongues were all shrivelled up, then we went down for the remaining three and after going (without lights) some 100 yards we stumbled on another man who proved to be the owner of the mines, Mr Dugdale, and we got him out. Just as we got to the top of the pit there was another explosion and after waiting half an hour we went down again and got out two others, quite dead, then we knew the rest of the men and boys could not possibly be alive so we closed them in and shut up the pit.

'It was the most sickly sight to be imagined. My arms were covered with large pieces of skin with flesh and blood on it and I was completely saturated with blood through carrying the men who, in the worst cases, were badly mangled and felt more like jelly than anything else. All have since died including the owner, the manager, and the two mining engineers. There does not seem to be a single woman in the district round who is not in mourning.'

There was a great deal of heroism over that weekend. Deputy Charles Day returned again and again, even when he knew his three sons had died of their injuries in the explosion. Day and three others received gold Albert Medals (only forty-five had been given up to that date), Fred Marsh was one of six other miners who received silver ones, and William Henry Sanders received a silver watch.

A great proportion of the newspaper reports of the time were taken up with progress reports on William Dugdale, his injuries and the doctors who attended on him. We learn that Dr Cromton, 'the eminent specialist from Birmingham', was sent for, arriving in Atherstone on the 5.48 p.m. train (those were the days . . .) and was met by two other doctors at the station. A blow-by-blow account was given of his condition until he died.

During the rest of the week, the injured miners were dying too. Many of them, unaware of the results of shock, had walked up to two miles home to their cottages before they collapsed. Without saline drips or modern methods of dealing with burns and internal injuries (or means of ascertaining such injuries), they died in great pain.

On 3 May all rescue attempts were abandoned and it was decided that the nine men still not found could not possibly have survived. The decision was taken to seal off the shaft and close down the pit. A report expresses surprise that the accident could ever have happened. 'The mine owners had described the pit as free from gas. Warwickshire pits were so free from gas that a naked candle could be used for purposes of illumination.'

At the inquest it was said that

'the various seams of coal in North Warwickshire have always been regarded as being of a less fiery nature than the coal which is procured in other parts of the country, and the absence of explosive gas in our pits has rendered it less necessary for those working in the bottoms to use those precautions with lights which are considered to be so highly essential in order to preserve life in fiery coal pits.'

There are some pathetic accounts from the resumed inquest, some time after it had been reopened. Eliza Blow deposed,

'I am a widow and the deceased, William Blow, was my husband. He was a miner. We lived at Grendon. I last saw him alive on the Monday night at about ten minutes past five. He worked the night shift at the colliery. I confirm the body in Coffin 1 is that of my husband. I recognised his clothes but I cannot recognise his features. I'm sure it is him. The knife produced is his and the pipe is like one he used to smoke.'

Another widow, Emma Ross, said,

'I am the widow of John Ross and I live on the Watling Street. My husband was a miner. He was about 40 years of age. I last saw him alive on Monday night at about five o'clock. I confirm that the body in Coffin 2 is that of my husband but I can recognise it by the teeth more than anything else. I cannot recognise the features. The tobacco box belonged to him and the knife be his. As well as his clothes was found a very worn piece of newspaper and some matches enclosed in a little bag. . . . A box contained four candles. He used to take four or five candles with him, not more. That night before going on shift he bumped his head and said he would be late at the mine. I said never mind. I do wish he'd been too late.'

Dr Hallsworth, the mine doctor, then described finding two bodies some time later behind a fall of coal, lying side by side and much decomposed. 'The bodies did not seem much injured nor were they burned. The clothes were partly covered in mould and partly in coal dust. I was then shown another body lying under a fall of coal. In my opinion the cause of death of the three men was suffocation caused by inhaling the noxious gases.

The inquest jury returned a verdict on the first twelve men who died in agreement with Dr Hallsworth's conclusions and went on to say,

'We consider it an error of judgment to have placed an engine and boiler so far from the bottom of the shaft in the return airway and in such an improper and unprotected manner so subjecting the pit to great risks and which was the cause of the fire.'

A report by Arnold Morley MP in 1884 to the House of Commons, as well as detailing what had taken place, drew attention to the jury's verdict and to the 'bad management of the mine'. In 1885, members of the Dugdale family brought an action at Birmingham Assizes against Francis Gillett, the consulting engineer and agent, winning a substantial £6,500 damages on the grounds that the engine had been improperly placed. Gillett, however, maintained that the fault lay altogether with John Parker, the certificated manager of the mine. So the mine owners blamed the agent who blamed the manager who was unable to blame anybody since he had died in the rescue attempt to reach the trapped miners.

It was twelve months before the pit could reopen. During subsequent weeks, the plug put on to seal off the mouth of the shaft blew off several times. Nearly 400 men found themselves without work and a fund was set up to help the victims' families but as is often the case with these things, there were bitter recriminations and much contention. Some temporary relief had been given by the Board of Guardians as it had been stated at the inquest that the miners' wages had been so low that no provision could possibly have been made to meet the wants caused by the accident. Pay sheets from Baddesley thirty years later showed take home pay of £1. 7s. 0d., £1. 4s. 9d., 13s. 6d., £1. 5s. 6d., and so on.

A year later a poem was circulating by an anonymous poet about little girls found selling flowers on Nuneaton market, some 7 miles away, to buy food for their families. It is Victorian poetry at its worst but it details the story of the disaster as it affected one family and, after due praise for the Dugdale family, continues:

> Now he's gone there's little comfort in our home at
>   Baxterley,
> But the worst's not told you yet, Ma'am, for we're
>   penniless you see.
> That's my tale and now I'm trying with these flowers
>   father grew
> To support my widowed mother and my little sisters, too.

The people in the area have not forgotten and the centenary of the disaster, in 1982, was marked by church services and a special exhibition. They remembered the disaster, the heroism of those who risked or gave their own lives to save their comrades and also the poverty, near-starvation and suffering which followed afterwards.

4

Baddesley miners

David Smalley lived in a small terraced cottage in the village of Sheepy Magna, just outside the town of Atherstone where he was born. He was a tiny, bird-like man with an enormous sense of humour and a dry wit. Until the last few months of his life he had his own seat in the 'local' to which he repaired at the same time every evening. He had not worked for a considerable time — he was 74 when he died — suffering from angina and from chronic chest problems. He was a well-known local story teller.

'Of course Atherstone town is so different now you wouldn't recognise it. We was all living in "the yards" as they were called in them days, the houses were built round them like. There were Polly Cook's Yard and King's Yard. We lived in King's Yard with the bank one side, the police station the other and Fuller's shop at the front. As a lad I used to be sent out to buy a bucket of small ale for the old folks. The White Bear Inn used to brew its own beer and you'd take up a couple of those big enamel buckets on a yoke and he'd fill you up each bucket for 1½ pence.

'The old men and women would be sitting out in the yards of a summer's night smoking their pipes — men and women smoked the old clay pipes — and you'd start at one end of the yard with your bucket and they'd scoop out the beer with an old tin mug and by the time you got to the top of the yard it had all gone and they'd send you back again for more.

'Mind you beer was only 2 pence a pint in those days and do
you know there was twenty-seven pubs in Atherstone then!
They said if you had drunk a dessertspoonful of ale in the first
pub, and two in the second you'd be dead drunk before you'd
got to the end of them all — nobody ever finished them so far
as I know.'

The pub names list like a directory of public house names –
The King's Head, The White Hart, The White Bear, The
Wheatsheaf, The Bell, The George and Dragon, The Boar Inn,
The Bluebell, The Black Boy, The Three Tuns, The Old Red
Lion, The White Horse, The Woolpack, The Coach and Horses,
The Beaver, The Black Horse, The Dolphin, The New Swan,
The Bull's Head, The Shanghai, The King's Arms, The Angel,
The Maid of the Mill, The Cricketers' Arms, The Woodman,
The Royal Oak were there in fairly recent memory. One can
only marvel at how they all made a living.

'By hell, they'd drink though, especially on a Friday. I've
seen the colliers going back on shift of a Saturday morning still
in their pit dirt from the night before.

'The workhouse was still going then. They pulled it down
later and made it into a cinema. They'd give you some kind of
a bed for the night in it and in exchange you'd to cut sticks for
kindling and tie them into bundles. Then they'd give you a
breakfast and out you'd have to go, on the road and away.
There was poor old folks as had to live there, of course,
although it was always a last resort. Although it was in the
main street it had a great 14 foot wall round it, like it were a
prison.

'I was one of eleven children. My Mam lost two in infancy.
Times was very hard and my father he'd been in the hat
factory but it got there wasn't all that much work. He'd walk
miles and miles at harvest time, just to get a day's work. In the
end he went down the pit, though he hadn't wanted to. It was
all there was.

'All the pits round here were owned by Sir William Dugdale.
It was very different then to what it is now. Sir William's
manager would come around the schools as you got older and

take your name and when you got to 12 or so then your job was there waiting for you. You'd go down the same pit as your father. He were very strict were Sir William and you had to know your place. When his wife or family came by in the carriage the women had to come out and curtsey at the gate. If they didn't, their man could be laid off.

'I think I were about 13 when I started at the pit. Either you walked to work each day or sometimes you could catch the paddy engine at the wharf in Atherstone on the canal. It was a little steam train that came down from the pits to the canal to load the barges. The canal was very, very busy in them days, there was dozens of boats. Most of the traffic in and around this part went by canal and our canal was one of the busiest as it went to Coventry and linked up with the canals going to Birmingham and even up to London. Atherstone was a main stopping place for the boat people. There were stables on the canal side where they stabled their horses and they'd leave their horses there overnight and then get down to some serious drinking in the pubs.

'My first job was crab driver — yes *crab*. The crab were a small kind of an engine which pulled the tubs along. It were quite skilled work for a lad. Then I did other kinds of jobs and in the end they let me be Deputy's boy to my father who'd been made a Deputy.

'I never found old Lord Dugdale too bad an employer — though some did — it were them under him. The colliery manager were the biggest toe rag in the pit. Men still worked in teams then, under deputies, when I started. At the end of the week the money was shared out. At one time the men were taking 5s. out of our wages for "stoppages" — that is for paying it out and bothering with it. We was only getting 21s. all together. That got stopped in the end and different men used to do it different weeks. Compensation wasn't too good. You might get ten bob a week if you was badly injured. One man got killed in the pit when I was there and his family got £5 and were glad to get it. Of course, if you got laid off then there was nothing — absolutely nothing at all.

'There was two great times we looked forward to then — Atherstone Statutes and Shrove Tuesday. They used to say that Dugdale only wanted to give you the Tuesday of Statutes but had to give in and make it the Wednesday and all to give everyone a chance to get over Tuesday.

'There used to be stalls up the whole length of Long Street and out the back selling all manner of things. People would get together and have parties and club up and buy pork, beef and pickles. What money there was really got spent. The miners had their money and then there were quite a few hat factories in Atherstone in them days. It were famous for hats. Some men worked on the hats but a lot of women did too and the girls'd get jobs trimming them up.

'We used to go out into the country on the days off too. There was lots of tales about the place in my young days. They say there was underground passages from Merrivale Hall (where Dugdale lived) to Wharton and you could walk it all along a strip of ground which was over the tunnel. Then they said there was moor between the old nunnery at Polesworth and Pooley Hall. They said it were for the old nuns and monks in the old days to get out and have a bit of fun though perhaps it was just old coal mines.

'There'd been coal mines here a long time. They said the coal from Baddesley pit were the finest in the country, Baddesley Rider it were called. I remember the miners coming back from Baddesley on the paddy engine, desperate to get off and join in the ball game on a Shrove Tuesday.'

The Atherstone Ball Game still exists in a modified form and is very similar to the St Columb hurling in Cornwall, played on the same day, Shrove Tuesday, both games dating back far into the mists of antiquity. Both games are played up and down the street with a leather ball and no holds are barred. At Atherstone the 'winner' is he who has the ball at the end of the game and all kinds of subterfuges have been known in the way of hiding or 'smuggling' the ball as it is called. It is still a rough game but now lasts about two hours and is positively decorous compared to the old days.

'In the old times it would start at three o'clock and a woman would be called and she would kick out the ball. Then it was all hell, up and down the street — the shops were boarded up, of course. The ball would be taken down to each school and all the children would be allowed to kick it around for luck and then it would be kicked over the high wall into the workhouse and all those who could get about were allowed to kick it for half an hour and then it would have to be thrown back. They couldn't hang on to it in there, you see.

'Then up and down it would go and at the end of the afternoon the miners would join in, still in their pit dirt, wearing the pit boots and helmets, by Hell it were rough! I've seen chaps tossed into the canal. I remember once a chap from Baddesley pit got it and threw himself on a passing horse and cart and then went off hell for leather with it to Baddesley. Then there were the old woman who used to walk from Ratcliffe to Atherstone on market days and holidays with home-made butter in a straw bag and once she got jostled and pushed around and they got her out of the crowd and she went off home again. Then they found they'd lost the ball altogether and that night they knocked her up and there was the ball, squashed into the middle of a great blob of butter.

'In those days they used to pull the regular police out of Atherstone as it were a real day for settling old scores, the old poachers and whatnot would turn up just for the fight. They had to bring the policemen in from outside and there were still fights like you'd never believe. I've seen chaps running through the streets with all the clothes ripped off them and streaming blood.

'But they was decent on the whole. They didn't smuggle the ball till they were told they could. Then the search'd really begin. Chaps' coats and trousers'd come off, they come into your house if you hadn't locked it up and turn it inside out. Then the winner would get the ribbons. They'd tie a bunch of ribbons on the ball and he and his team would go round all the pubs and they'd make a collection. They still do it nowadays but now it's for charity.

'Life was hard. My father never earned much even though he were a Deputy in the end. But people were really friendly towards each other in those days, not like they are now. You had to rely on each other. Like if there were a fire. The engine was pulled by the same horses that pulled the hearse — you can imagine the problems. Sometimes they'd pull the hearse to church at a mad gallop and sometimes you'd find it going on

like a snail on its way to a fire. It took so long to tackle the
horses up the fire could be out before they ever got to it so the
whole town would turn out, passing buckets of water to each
other in a human chain to put out a fire.

'I saw nationalisation come into the pits and everything
changed there for the better, of course. You had some kind of
protection and security but I didn't enjoy it as long as I should
because they found I had angina and I had to give up. There's
a lot of bad health, of course, from working underground.

'One thing, however hard up miners were they always kept
pets of some kind. At one time I'd a budgie. He lived years and
years and I'd come in and say, "hello, you little bugger", and
he'd say, "hello, David, bin drinking again?" One morning he
didn't look right, kind of droopy. The wife said he'd been
chirping away quite brightly before. Anyhow, he eat his
breakfast and when I looked round he were dead on the floor
of the cage, poor little bugger. We never had another one —
you see, he were one of the family.'

Three or four miles away in the small mining village of
Dordon, Harry Horton lay in a bed in his clean sitting-room,
the oxygen mask always near at hand. The latter days of
miners are spent beside this particular piece of apparatus.

His account is short but supplements that of David Smalley.

'I started work at 14 and my first job was to work under the
conveyor belt which shook out the coal into different-sized
pieces and the dust just rained down on me, six days a week,
all day. I was told then that coal dust didn't hurt you. It was
even good for you, they said. Look at me now! Nobody had
heard of pneumoconiosis in Dugdale's pits and you should
look around now at those that are left, they've nearly all got
lung trouble or heart trouble or both.

'In the old days when I started if a man were injured then
his workmates were responsible for him. Dugdale didn't think
he'd any responsibility at all, no responsibility for any man or
any thing or for the safety of his workmen.

'The Dugdales were so mean they managed to stop the canal
from Atherstone getting any further than their own pit on their
own land for years, so that other peoples' coal couldn't be

transported along it and the price reduced. They did the same with the local railway line. The whole area was dependent on the Baxterley/Baddesley pits and everyone was, in some sense, employed by them – shopkeepers, landlords, pubs, everyone. After the disaster at Baxterley when all those chaps died the pit was sealed off for twelve months and my God, the families nearly starved to death.

'I was told that old Dugdale's son didn't go down there bravely to rescue his men like they put out afterwards. He was down there because he thought it was safe for him to go, seeing how quick he could get the men back on shift again. You see they'd already been up and told him once that there was something wrong and he told them to get back down there. The only memorial down there is to him – to nobody else at all. Men didn't matter. In his day miners were simply fodder for the industry.

'When the disaster threw everyone out of work, Parson Bacon started a scheme, digging up turf on the common and sowing vegetables but it didn't really work. There was a disaster fund but not much of it got through to those who needed it. When the last dependant died old Dugdale wanted to hand the money over to the British Legion for a club with a plaque to be put on it saying who had died but the National Union of Mineworkers objected and somehow or other that money just disappeared.

'The two best things that happened here were when the Warwickshire Miners and Mineworkers' Federation, "the Fed", were all incorporated into one strong national body, the NUM – and the other was nationalisation.

'But grim as it was and it was grim, the friendliness in the old days was wonderful. When a woman were confined they all took it in turn to do her washing, cook her husband's tea and the other kids' meals and they'd hold draws and collections for men out of work. They still do that for chaps that's got hurt or are sick.

'Baddesley colliery is a full-scale, modern working pit now. The part between it and the old Baxterley entrance where the disaster was is still sealed off to this day and there were two that were never found. I'd heard some funny stories about that pit but I'll tell you this one and it's the honest truth.

'One Sunday I was going down the main "road" in the pit when I met a chap coming up the other way. He said, "what time is it?" and I looked at my watch and told him. Then as I got past I suddenly thought — "Who's he?" "What's he doing down here and why isn't he wearing his lamp?" So I turned and followed after him as fast as ever I could and he kept steadily on in front of me and then he turned off at the old roadway to the end, where it is still all sealed off from the disaster — and he disappeared. Straight through the wall. He honestly did, he just kept on walking.

'They do say that some people have seen the Deputy's boy down there too, carrying the lamp.

'There's a lot of stories you remember though. I remember the chap they called "Trammangle". He was called that because when he were young and poor he bought an old wooden mangle at a sale in Atherstone. He pushed it all the way home to Baddesley on a pram and the miners said he were "tramming a mangle" and so he were known as "Trammangle" ever afterwards.

'Then there was the famous murder. There was an overman thought his wife were unfaithful. He gave in his tally down the pit at North Warwick, went underground on foot 8 miles into the Armington pit, came up there, walked to his house and killed his wife and then went back down and on shift and came up again just as if nothing had happened. You can go the whole way down levels and roads, from pit to pit, and never meet another soul.

'In spite of what happened to me I still think the mining communities are the best places in the world. Like I said, if you were sick or your wife confined they'd all turn out. That's why miners are like they are. There's still some of it left. People miss it when they go out of the pit into other industries where it's dog eat dog. It's never been like that down in the pit — you see it can't be.'

5

Working the slate

The tiny slate mining town of Blaenau Ffestiniog in North Wales lies in an extremely dramatic situation, hanging in a narrow pointed peak. Below the town, the Machno Valley falls steeply away to the sea at Port Madoc, the port built specially to export slate. It is still linked to Blaenau by the old narrow gauge railway. The town itself, virtually a single road of shops and cottages, climbs steeply upwards, winding its way towards the massive slate mines and quarries which bear witness to the size and scale of past industry. Below these vast heaps of slate, in the cemetery, row upon row of slate gravestones bear another kind of witness — to the men of Blaenau who died young of the dust from working the slate.

The slate industry of North Wales dates back to the early 1700s and it did not become established until long after Cornish slate from Delabole and Pembroke slate from further west were keeping whole communities. Yet by the mid-1700s it was a prime export — for example during the eighteen months from June 1729 to December 1730 over 2,500,000 slates were sent out from the small ports along the North Wales coast. At its peak the industry employed over 16,700 men, nearly a quarter of them working at the nineteen mines and quarries around Blaenau. Virtually everybody in towns like Blaenau and the villages further north around Penrhyn worked the slate. Apart from a little farming there was nothing else.

Beneath the real mountains which tower over Blaenau and those made of discarded slate, lie level upon level of caverns, some 200 feet high, where the men have brought out the slate for two hundred years. The entire landscape is dominated and scarred by the workings. Below the level of green growth on the mountains, everything is grey. Slate is everywhere — in the walls, on the roofs, facing houses; you cannot get away from it. In the hot weather a continual fine dust still rises from the quarries; when it is wet the sense of greyness from the all-pervading mountains of loose slate is overpowering, even though the slate industry has now dwindled away to virtually nothing.

Slate working in Blaenau began in 1755 when Methusalem Jones came over from Nantlle — where there were already quarries — to look for slate at Blaenau, guided, it is said, by a dream. He and five others worked the first slate mine, Diffwys. After that the full exploitation of the area was left to the English using Welsh labour. Early slate mine owners include people like William Turner who came from Lancashire. In 1830 the 23-year-old son of a Warwick banker, John Whitehead Greaves, left home to seek fame and fortune and turned his attention to Blaenau. Joined by a Worcester man, Edwin Shelton, he leased two slate quarries from the then landowner, Lord Newborough, and set about building up a business in slate. It was a slow business and by the time Shelton died, in 1848, the profits were still very small. However Greaves kept doggedly on and a year later, in 1849, a team of men working for nothing blasted a tunnel into the mountain side above Blaenau and found one of the richest slate veins ever found in the country, now known as the Merioneth Old Vein.

It was to make Greaves a fortune. Eventually the mining on that site at Llechwedd spread over sixteen floors of workings, going down to a depth of 1000 feet, with as many as thirty caverns being worked on each level. The technique used underground, leaving pillars of slate and rock to support the chambers above, was the same used centuries before below Jerusalem when the stone was mined for Solomon's temple. During the heady days of the slate industry, the nineteenth century, William Madocks built the port of Port Madoc on the Dwyryd estuary especially to export slate from Blaenau and by

1872 the rail link had been completed. But from the turn of the century the decline was rapid. The demand for slate fell away – with two small peaks after the First and Second World Wars – and also there was a great deal of unrest in the workforce. Earnings were poor and the system of payment meant that many workers were forced into debt. In 1893 there was a major dispute at Llechwedd which lasted sixteen weeks.

In spite of modern technology tools for working the slate have changed little over the years. The basic two for splitting the slate are a broad, thin chisel and a wooden hammer bound with iron. In the early days the splitter then passed the slates on to a dresser who trimmed them to the right size by hand, using a special knife, but later the trimming was done by machine.

As traditional as the tools are the names the slate workers give to the various sizes of finished slate. The names first appeared in the Penrhyn mines and quarries but were later adopted universally. They range from the largest slate – the empress, which is 26" x 8". In a booklet on Llechwedd Slate Mine, Ivor Wynne quotes a poem written by a visiting judge in the nineteenth century:

It has been said, as we all must deplore,
That Granville and Pitt have made peers by the score,
But now 'tis asserted, unless I have blundered,
There's man that makes peeresses here by the hundred.
This countess or lady though crowds may be present,
Submits to be dressed by the hands of a peasant,
And you'll see, when her grace is but once in his clutches,
With how little respect he will handle a duchess.

The slate industry has left Blaenau Ffestiniog behind as it has Penrhyn and Nantlle, leaving behind it a great blight of waste land and a string of ghost villages. Along the main street of Blaenau it looks as if every other house is for sale.

The great Llechwedd Mine has now become a tourist attraction as a slate museum. Trains take holidaymakers down to the next-to-deepest level below ground so that they can see where the men worked and to what depth. Trams take others overground through the vast surface caverns where waxwork figures of slate workers can be seen blasting, drilling and loading the slate into waggons. There are exhibitions showing how slate is split, dressed and cut, with photographs of the old days and records of accidents — many workers lost their lives or were injured from slate or stone falling on them while they worked. In the mill it is possible to see slate still being worked although now it is to make the souvenirs, such as the exquisite fine slate fans, that visitors want to take away with them. On a fine day thousands of people pass through Llechwedd to look and marvel at the sheer size of the workings and to try and imagine what it was like in the old days. But it is difficult to be unaware of what the slate did to those who worked it. The fine, mica-laden dust of slate brings in its wake silicosis. It is insidious. Even now a man can be retired with 20 per cent disability to find, five years later, that it has crept up to 80 per cent. As long ago as 1848 it was suspected that the fine dust was entering the workers' lungs and causing a dreadful, early death. It was not until 1979 that legislation was passed to enable slate workers to claim compensation for what their job had done to them as can coal miners. Yet even now it can be difficult for an old slate worker to convince the necessary medical panel that he is suffering from silicosis.

Men who know they have the symptoms of the disease are told it is chronic bronchitis and in some cases it is only after they are dead that a post mortem proves they were right. Those familiar with the attitude taken towards the workers in the coalfields and asbestos industries will not be surprised to learn that as late as 1922 the North Wales Slate Quarry Proprietors' Association published widely the opinion of the Penrhyn quarry doctor who said, 'I am convinced after four years' experience here that slate dust is not merely harmless but beneficial.' Yet whether the men worked the 'bargain' system, described later, or whether they were simply employed on piece work the earnings were always very low. The workers never earned a good living from slate.

Len Owen, who now works at Llechwedd as a guide, looks ageless, a very gentle, softly-spoken Welsh man with a musical voice and a fine courtesy. He spoke to me sitting on a high platform, right above the Llechwedd mine to which we had climbed up a steep flight of crumbling slate steps. Below lay the huge mounds of discarded slate, massive pieces flung together like discarded building blocks. Behind us were crumbling old buildings from the mine, now disused and twisted, rusty machinery, old wire ropes, silent trolleys and enormous wheels.

Far below again, tourists crawled all over the site, some waiting in queues for the railway trains or trams, others clambering around the lower slopes of the slate mountains.

Floating up to us came the sound of the trains taking parties of tourists down to the lower levels or into the mine caverns, an endless squeak and rattle of wheels on rails while further up the hill a solitary dumper truck chugged away clearing slate rubble. A hot sun shone down on us; it was so dry drifts of slate dust hung everywhere. 'Would you believe me,' said Len, 'if I told you it was always sunny in Blaenau?' He worked at Llechwedd slate mine as did his father and grandfather before him.

'Not only did they work here but also my brothers, uncles, cousins as well — you see there was nothing else here to do. My grandfather came here from Anglesey. My grandmother was a Blaenau girl who was in service just near the Menai Bridge and they met over there and he came back here with her and there was only the quarry work for him to do. Before that he had worked on farms.

'My father he started at Llechwedd when he was 12 years old. He started as a labourer, what they called a "rubbisher". That was how they all had to start. Then you would ask to be promoted to rockman and my father was a rockman for many, many years.'

Most of the men at Llechwedd worked on the 'bargain' system. This had some similarities with the Cornish tin tributers but whereas the tributers and the mine owners took a gamble on the richness of the possible ore, the slate owners had a fair idea of where the best veins lay. The 'bargain' was made between a team of four, with sometimes an apprentice as a fifth, and a four-week month was worked. At the start of it the team leader and the owners' agent would agree on a working price for the rock in a particular chamber, the better the quality or the easier it was to extract, the lower the price. Poor or difficult rock fetched higher prices. The bargain bound the slate workers in the same way the tin **tributers** were bound but the team's pay was governed by the output of finished slate checked at the end of each month. Slate workers never had the opportunity to earn the money a lucky tribute man might should he strike a rich lode at a time when tin was fetching a high price.

As Len says,

'the rockmen would go down into the chambers and blast the rock to reach the slate and then get the blocks of slate up to the mill outside. Once they went to the mill they were cut and then split and dressed to whatever thickness was required and then they were ready for a roof. It was a highly skilled job. Of the four men in a bargain, two would be rockmen and two would be splitting. At the end of each month the money they had earned was divided between them. During that time you would have to live on a "sub" from the management, a loan until you got your month's pay. I can remember when it was £1. 13s. a week for a rubbisher and £1. 16s. for a rockman or a splitter, just after the 1914-18 war.

'My own first wage was 5s. and do you know, it never left my hand until I got home, I was so scared of losing it. It went down on the kitchen table and my mother said, "here's 3d. for your lunch and 1d. for the tin", the penny was savings you see. Always a penny in the box to save.

'How much they earned depended a lot on chance and what chamber you were in. You did stand a better chance of a higher wage working on the Old Vein than if you were in the Back Chamber with a harder rock. It took a long time, you see, just to clear the rock away to get at the slate but the Old Vein was so rich you'd be into the money straight away.

'I started in the way most boys did. My father knew I'd soon be leaving school when I got to 14, so he told his team about two or three months before it happened and see if they thought they could take on an apprentice. Then they would look after me and I'd get sent slates from that particular chamber to split and dress and cut. You'd be working on your

own but the men would look after you and you'd be taught
how to do it step by step. You learned by actually doing the job
and it took some learning. You couldn't learn it before you
came up here. You'd visit the mine, of course, and see the men
working in the chambers and probably watch your dad at work
but you didn't know how to do it. It took some time to get the
hang of it, the knack. It would take anything from five to seven
years to do it properly. Nowadays youngsters can do it in two
or three but they were much stricter in the old days.

'A good splitter then, working on slate from the Old Vein,
could split it very thin. The normal width of a roofing slate is
one eighth of an inch but you could split the Old Vein as thin
as a thirty-second of an inch if you were really skilled.

'They never earned much money. When I started it was
6s. 4d. a day and then it went up to about 8s. 4d. and the
Llechwedd was very fair compared to many quarries, even my
father said they were fair about the wages. When I started the
manager at the Oakley quarry (where I worked) was very
good. I would have to go over to the office in the morning as I
would fetch the post from the post office and take it up to the
mine office and being as I was in the children's choir, and a
soloist, we'd very often be having rehearsal two or three times
a week or a concert, so I would take off my cap and knock on
the door and ask if I could go home early and he'd always say
"yes" but he'd say "but don't come back unless you have had
an encore". Sometimes I did, very often, in fact — but
sometimes I didn't and I'd always tell him even though he had
said if I didn't get an encore he wouldn't let me go again.

'Sundays were very religious. There'd be Chapel in the
morning, Sunday school in the afternoon, Chapel again at
night and then, if you were in the choir like me, then it would
be choir practice after Chapel.

'So the boys would go into the quarry and the only thing for
the girls was for them to go into service. Parents would find
them a job in service because that was all there was. They'd go
perhaps to one of the few farms or more often to the houses of
the higher-up kind of people but there weren't many of them
so more often than not they would have to go away to work —
and for hardly any money — and they'd be staying there and
perhaps only getting home once a fortnight or once a month.

'What I do remember from the old days was how crowded it was when we all lived together. You all lived as a family in a very small house, your parents and perhaps your grandfather, your own brothers and then your uncles as well and if it had been a bad day, raining all the time, your mother would have all the clothes around the fire drying for the following morning. I can remember as if it were yesterday the steam around the old fireplace.

'I can tell you too from Monday to Friday what we had for dinner, every day. On the Sunday, you see, we would have had the special dinner, lamb or mutton, so on Monday you had the rest of what you didn't eat on Sunday there on the table for Monday's dinner. On Tuesday we'd have what you would call soup but we called here "lobscowse" made from what was left. That was how mother managed, by spreading the meat along over the week. Then Wednesday and Thursday we'd have potatoes baked in the oven and she'd boil up some carrots and onions and after that there'd be rice pudding, not much, but a bit for everyone. On Friday you'd go out down to the chip shop with a big bowl to carry away and 1s. filled that bowl to overflowing with chips and if there was money over there'd be perhaps one piece of fish between two or four of you. There wasn't much luxury around here.

'Mind you prices are different. I remember once talking to an old gentleman called Henry Parry and he told me that there used to be a tailor lived in the town in Low Street when he was a young man and a quarry man who wanted a suit would go to his house in the morning before going to work. He'd be measured and when he came back at night, at six o'clock, the suit would be ready and all for 5s. Five shillings! Or as old Henry put it, "for two half crowns. . . ."

'This was a very close community in the old days. When you were working in the quarry if you needed anything, a tool or anything at all, all you had to do was to go into the next chamber where the other men were working and they'd lend you anything. Then if you were sick or had an accident they'd have a concert for you in the town and the proceeds would go to the family concerned. When there was a bit extra it was shared and my mother told me that when she was in service with the Rev. J.W. Roberts he would give her a basket of bits and pieces and she would go to the town to those in trouble and there'd always be something, even if it was only a piece of butter or some sugar.

'We had to be self-educated then. We used the library and you had to sign for the books when you took them out but nobody could afford to buy books then. There were no cheap paperback books or anything like that. But we did buy the newspapers and periodicals. It only cost a penny for a newspaper then.

'My own interest like many others around here was singing and I'm a member still of the Moelwyn Male Voice Choir. When you are in a choir like that you really learn to sing. There is one song I don't think any choir in the world sings like the Moelwyn. It was written by a man who lived here in the early days who had to move away and in it he remembers the mountains and he says that there is no place like home and no place like Wales, of course. But our most famous song is called "Speed Your Journey" and when we have sung it abroad — and we were the first Welsh choir to go to Iceland and we have been to Brittany, Holland and Germany — people tell us we sing from the heart.

'Yes, our family has suffered much from the dust. My uncle for instance, died at 48 years of age of the silicosis and the lung cancer. Then my father worked in the open. There were two kinds of chambers and he worked in an open one which was open all the time to the winter rain and the snow. He'd take an old sack and put it around his shoulders and put some sacking on his legs to protect him from the weather. By the time he finished in the mine he was a total cripple. At the end he couldn't even put on his socks and shoes or even wash his feet and I used to do that for him because I was the youngest. He was crippled by the rheumatism and arthritis caused by the wet.

'There were two hospitals near here. If you went into the one in Carnaervon it meant you were not too bad yet. The other was at Abergele and you knew if you were transferred from Carnaervon to Abergele then there would be no chance at all for you to survive. Once the dust had really got to your lungs then that was that — finished.

'It is terrible to think that it is only about two or three years since they started paying out the compensation. It is no real compensation, though, to the widows whose men have died — they would rather have the men here and alive. Yet they always worked so hard. In Blaenau they never striked except for the General Strike in 1926 and not many industries had such a good record, did they?

'I have four children, two of them sons. No, they didn't want to go into slate even if they could have done. My eldest drove a train here for the visitors for a while but then he went away as he's a mechanic. My other son is a carpenter and joiner. Generations change but I don't believe those who say the younger generation don't want to work. The young people here are desperate for work and they can't get it. They go away and now they can't even get work anywhere else either and they have to come back here for nothing.

'People say to me wouldn't it upset the old men to see the tourists coming here to this quarry and mine but to me it does show how the old men did work. Mind you, I don't think they would like it but they wouldn't say much. But I think it's a good thing to show what it was really like — you don't hear much about the slate, it's all the time the coal miners.

'In this place of Blaenau it's a slow-running life, no rush at all. We like to greet everybody, no matter who they are or what nationality they are. I could never stop and pass anyone in the street without passing the time of day and asking how they are. There was a man moved into our street from Manchester and he was very surprised when I came out one morning — I'd found out his name — and I said, "Good day to you, Bob, and how are you?" He found it odd at first but then he thought it was much nicer our way.'

I had met Kate Roberts three years earlier, in 1979, when she was 88 and living in a quiet house in a cul-de-sac in Denbigh. She was still a formidable presence and was somewhat amused at having just been 'discovered' as a novelist. The discovery had been made only after some of her novels had been translated into English — she had been famous in her own language for years.

She is indeed a rarity. The daughter of a slate worker who did not follow the only road for a girl as recalled by Len Owen, that of service with a big family. She actually broke with the past and had a career though she has never forgotten her roots and her books describe the life of the working-class families — and especially the women — in loving detail.

Her background is from the area north of Blaenau.

'My father was a crofter and a quarryman in Snowdonia. He started work at the age of 9, as an apprentice in the Penrhyn quarries learning how to split the slate, learning as he went along.

'In those days the men sold their labour — so many slates for so much — and he generally worked in a "bargain" group. It was a very hard life indeed and the men never knew until the end of a month what the owners were going to pay.'

At least the Cornish tributers knew the price of their 'set' before they ever commenced work on it.

'Often the bargain in the quarries where my father worked was a very poor one — but it was that or nothing at all. If the place allotted to them to work was a good one and the rock easy to handle then all they could expect was a low price. If it was otherwise then they might get a better price but only at the beginning of a month. Often they had to accept the low price and on top of that, they knew that the man who inspected the slates at the end of the month would discard more slates as being faulty than was true, if the market was weak.

'My father's brother was killed in the quarry. He was only 10 years old at the time and they didn't find his body for a month. My mother had a little schooling and then she went into service when she was 10 years old. I was the child of a second marriage. My father had three boys and he was 40, my mother had one son and she was 36. Then there was myself and some more brothers — a large family in hard times.

'But it would be wrong to think there was no cultural life in the slate communities. Families read everything they could lay their hands on although it was a limited choice as most of them spoke only Welsh. We had five weekly newspapers coming into our cottage and all kinds of magazines. My mother grumbled endlessly about the cost — and read them all avidly.

Much of our life revolved around the Chapel, not just services, but literary and music festivals, poetry, writing competitions.'

At 11 Kate did a remarkable thing. She won a scholarship to the county school, virtually unknown for a girl.

'My mother really didn't want me to go. She thought I should stay home and help her but my father persuaded her. I just don't know how they managed. A good earning month for my father was £5 and although I had a scholarship they had to pay for lodgings for me in Carnaervon, my books and stationery. But we never starved as we were lucky enough to grow our own vegetables and had our own milk and eggs.

'Then I won another scholarship to university in Bangor and I took Latin and History and Welsh. In those days you had to take compulsory philosophy too and you can imagine the effect it had on the rest of the family. In 1904 I got a first class honours degree.' She was proud of being not only the first woman in Wales to graduate but that she did so long before Oxford awarded degrees to women in England. Writers like Dorothy Sayers, for example had to wait until after the 1914-18 war to graduate.

'Wales had more respect, you see, for education and even then a better attitude for women going on to it if they could. After that it had to be teaching. However well qualified you were, you started in the primary schools as I did at £60 a year and it was only when the First World War took away all the men that I was able to get a job in a secondary school at double the money, £120. I met my husband Morris at a summer school. He was a printer and together we bought a small printing works.'

Finally they ran a weekly newspaper together until he died in 1946.

There is a lot of Kate Roberts's own mother in her novel, *Feet in Chains*. As its title suggests, she draws heavily on her own background and the difficulty for slate workers of breaking from it and many of the incidents she writes about happened in reality. The woman of the novel, wife to a slate worker, is intelligent and lives a life far below her natural potential but she lives it without rancour or sentimentality. It is her children who feel their feet chained by circumstances and by the environment of the slate quarries and mines.

Of her father's generation she says,

'this was a generation that came to take an interest in the plight of the worker. They gathered their ideas from English books or from the Welsh papers that echoed the English ones. The worker in Wales came to be recognised along with his counterpart in England. It was the same problem in every country, with the same enemy — capitalism. In the old days some of the quarries had been worked by the quarrymen themselves, sharing the profits.'

Many of the younger people, she says, turned away from the conventional nonconformist religion with its devotion and self-sacrifice.

'The young felt there had been too much self-sacrifice. Their interest in politics was partisan. The old and middle-aged were Radicals before they believed that was best for the workers. They regarded the Tory party as the ruling class whose sole object was to keep the workers down.'

Yet, she says, it was very difficult to get the slate men to join the unions of quarrymen. 'It was useless to try and persuade the workers they would never be able to negotiate a minimum wage agreement without a strong union.'

Her life has made her an ardent Welsh Nationalist although she does not agree with the kind of violence which leads to burning down cottages. 'Welsh Nationalism has given us dignity again. The English have left a bitter legacy in the slate country.'

In *Feet in Chains*, she recollects, she draws on two true stories which show just what brought about the legacy. One concerns a woman whose son has been fighting in France during the 1914-18 war. She is waiting for a letter from him and rushes to the postman when he whistles at her gate. He hands her a long brown envelope with an official stamp on it. She thinks it must be some kind of Government form and opens it but as it is in

English she cannot read it so she takes it along to the local shop to ask the English-speaking shopkeeper to read it to her.

After holding it in his hand for a while he begins to speak. Says Kate Roberts, 'you see it was to say her son had been killed and he had to tell her. All over Wales women were receiving that kind of letter or telegram − in English. It never occurred to them to put it into Welsh.'

Hard as the life was for the wives and children of slate workers there was, at least, some money coming into the home. Where the breadwinner had died in the trenches there was nothing and, as a young woman, Kate had seen what happened to the families afterwards. Mothers of apprentices in the slate quarries were supposed to be entitled to some kind of compensation, or a pension, if the boy was killed in the war and a surviving son asks for such compensation for his mother.

An English official arrived with forms in English. He wants to know what the boy earned at the quarry, what the other children earn − if anything − how much does the woman make off her bit of land, for how much does she sell her eggs and vegetables? Then he said he could do nothing − she had far too much money coming in.

He then told her that he had just reduced the pension of the widow living nearby from 12s. a week to 8s. as she can make a bit of money selling eggs. The woman to whom he was speaking was so enraged she hit him on the head with a broom.

Kate Roberts's escape from the hard life of a quarryman's daughter was almost unique in her day and age. A group of admirers of her work raised the money and bought the small croft where she was born in Snowdonia and are restoring it.

'They have now put the roof back on and put a small plaque on the wall saying I was born there. I find that very moving. My family would have been very proud.'

Kate Roberts's main legacy is a written record of the lives of those thousands who worked the slate and lived and died, unrecorded and unheard, in the slate mines and quarries of North Wales.

PART 2

COASTAL WATERS

6

Singing the fishing

For centuries the sea provided a living all around the coast of the British Isles for those hardy enough to seek it. From the north of Scotland, along the east coast with the great ports of Hull, Grimsby, Great Yarmouth and Lowestoft, down to the west country and Newlyn, Mousehole and St Ives, up again to Wales and then to the north west and Fleetwood, men hauled and trawled the harvest of the sea.

Nearer inshore were the cheaper shellfish and, in one or two fortunate spots, oysters. In West Wales cockles provided a living for some while on the fast-flowing Welsh rivers the coracle men netted salmon in a manner which had not changed in three thousand years.

In its heyday fishing provided a host of small ancillary occupations and industries. The Scottish herring girls followed the fleets along the coast, gutting and storing the herring, while their counterparts in Cornwall did the same with the pilchards. In Lowestoft men, women and girls made by hand the huge nets needed for the bigger boats. Whole communities were built entirely around the industry.

First under sail, then steam, then diesel, the boats would set off both for the great far-off fishing grounds and also for those in our prolific coastal waters. In the summer the great shoals of pilchards arrived off Cornwall and the tiny ports were crammed with boats. It was said you could walk from side to side of Newlyn Harbour on fishing boats.

Off Scotland and the east coast were the great shoals of herring, caught by the thousands of tons. Even when both pilchards and herring had long since disappeared there were still huge shoals of mackerel. The winter shoal was truly enormous, often stretching in the western waters from Looe, just south of Plymouth, right around Land's End — 50 miles and upwards. It was several miles across and hundreds of feet deep.

This is no longer the case. First to disappear were the pilchards. Whether they were overfished or suddenly changed their habits has been a matter of dispute by experts for years, but opinion is now coming down hard in favour of overfishing, in view of subsequent events.

Next to disappear were the shoals of herring, not only overfished in the mature shoals but fished out of existence by the big trawlers who actually trawled the spawning grounds. After years of banning herring fishing, numbers are slowly beginning to creep up but east coast fishermen say bitterly that the Danes are still trawling up tiny herring. The east coast fishing fleets have dwindled away; the latest-built and most modern trawlers being sold abroad. There has been little to replace the industry in those areas which relied upon it and the only regular employment now is fishing for the small amount of white fish which goes to the processed food industry in the form of products like fish fingers.

Last to go has been the mackerel although warning lights were flashing for at least ten years. Mackerel had been an underrated fish, always plentiful but difficult to keep and store. By the late 1970s it had become the only fish capable of being fished in quantity off our shores and to the coastal waters of Britain came the huge east European factory ships, and deep sea trawlers from as far afield as France, Denmark, Norway, Belgium, Holland, Iceland, even Egypt. Desperate for a living, these were joined by the remnants of the Scottish and east coast trawler fleets developed for fishing in quantity much further afield. Local inshore fishermen sent frantic appeals to the Government for help to receive in return soothing reassurances that the mackerel quota fixed by Whitehall experts was perfectly satisfactory. There were still plenty of fish.

The inshore fishermen disagreed. It was obvious, anyway, that the quota system was being blatantly disregarded. Deep sea trawlers regularly fished inside the 3 mile limit, clearly visible to watchers on the shore. Visible to those at sea were the smaller boats, loading one catch of mackerel on to the factory ships out of sight of land, then bringing in a second catch as their quota to the fish market. The fishermen began to go bankrupt.

Nor is it just coastal fishing which is rapidly nearing extinction.

Interference with the waterways, pollution and, again, commercial fishing has affected the salmon and the lives of the fast-dwindling number who fish them on a small scale. The famous oyster beds of the Fal which had provided a living for at least two thousand years have, by 1982, had to be closed half way through the season to try and preserve what is left. The only growth industry is in crabs and one wonders how long that can stand the enormous numbers now taken out of the sea.

The effects extend far outside the problems of the fishermen. The small communities were built around the fleets. Little villages and towns, tightly packed around their harbours or along estuaries and coves, had a lifestyle based on that one industry. Life had been virtually unchanged for centuries, change only being marked by the arrival of such amenities as electricity and piped water, along with faster methods of getting the fish away to inland markets. The larger boats acquired more sophisticated equipment, such as echo sounders and radar.

Now it is fast being swept away. On the Cornish cliffs there are now only the ruins of the 'huers' ' huts. The huer was the man who looked out for the shoals from the high cliffs and signalled to the boats where to go. Guided by the huer signalling with bundles of rags from the shore, they could find where the shoal was thickest and as the huer guided in the first boats, so the second wave would be waiting. The old sailing luggers could sail weighed down with fish to less than eighteen inches of freeboard and it is said they could sail closer to the wind than any other ship afloat.

The pilchard lofts described in the accounts that follow have become bijou summer residences for holidaymakers. The net lofts on the east coast either lie empty and boarded up or have been pulled down. Fishermen's cottages all around the coast have become second homes or summer lets, often standing empty for nine or ten months of the year while a rash of new building around some of the towns and villages has brought in a new population, heavily weighted in favour of retired, old people who cannot bring new growth or industry with them.

Young people with nowhere to live move away. For those who remain catches are so small they do not even recoup the amount spent on diesel fuel putting out to sea. At the end of a piece I wrote for the *New Statesman* in January 1980, I described the huge harbour extension built at Newlyn at a cost of around £2 million and how local fishermen said it had come far too late.

So, after the pilchards there were herring; after the herring, mackerel. But after the mackerel? There is nothing. By the end of December 1981 virtually all mackerel fishing had been banned off the coast of Britain except for small inshore boats. Even the holiday industry on which many of the coastal villages have relied instead is suffering as a result of general recession.

What follows in subsequent chapters are the reminiscences of those who were involved in the fishing, some now in their eighties and nineties, some younger. From the west country come the accounts of John Jack Pender of Mousehole and his late wife, Nettie, and Joe Tonkin of Newlyn. From the river Fal are the memories of 89-year-old Henry Merrifield, oysterman, and today's viewpoint from the Truro harbour master, Captain Whitehouse. From the port of Lowestoft on the east coast are the memories of George Crisp's father, William, of Frank Fisk of Lowestoft and of Jessie Thacker, netmaker. From Wales comes the story of the struggle for survival of today's coracle fishermen and, from the past, the story of Llanstephan, its cockles and the colliers who used to spend their holidays in the village recovering from their life underground.

Only the crab fishermen have an optimistic story to tell. For the rest, there is a pessimistic unanimity of outlook over a situation which the old men and women say has been brought about by man's greed.

John Jack Pender lives in the cottage in Mousehole where his family has lived for hundreds of years. He will tell you his great-great-many-times-great-grandfather fought the Spaniards when they landed and burned Mousehole in 1596. His small sitting-room is crowded with a lifetime's souvenirs and many paintings of boats – some by his own father who turned to painting in his retirement, others by his son, Jack, a professional painter. John Jack was 91 when he talked to me and hearty and vigorous. He was still winning cups as a yacht skipper when he was 80.

He is an almost legendary figure locally and before her death, his wife Nettie used to be much in demand at local Women's Institutes and meetings of the Old Cornwall Society because of her splendid memory for the old days of Mousehole village.

'We had a little new pilchard boat when I was a boy and I'd go out in it when I came home from school. It was sailed with two hands and a boy. That's what the days were like then, school in the day and the sea at night and you'd rarely be in before midnight.

'I remember coming in from school one night and my mother said I didn't have to go to sea because Dad had gone to Penzance on business but I didn't like to lose a night so I went out on the front and saw a chap doing nothing and asked him if he'd go to sea with me for the night and he said he would. I went aft and took the tiller and we shot the nets and got the pilchards. I couldn't bear the idea of losing a night. But you'd end up very tired in the school the next day and I remember the schoolmaster kicking me in the shin to wake me up. . . .

'When I was 13 the schoolmaster told us the leaving age was going up to 14 so anyone who wanted to leave must do so now – my hand was the first up. I had a berth waiting for me, you see, on one of the big mackerel boats. They had six hands and a boy and I was the boy.

'My first boat was the *Humility* out of Mousehole. In the winter we went up to Scarborough and Lowestoft on the herring fishing. They were sailing boats then, of course. We still fished entirely under sail. Sometimes it'd take three days and nights to get there, sometimes it might take a week. It were all drifting in them days — in the fishing the one season followed the other, pilchards, then the summer mackerel, then herring drifting in the winter from mid-November 'til around Christmas, then down on the herrings still to Plymouth. It was sometimes good, sometimes bad but always better than it is today.

'From Christmas to February we fished off Plymouth's Big Bury Bay Banks and they never failed. While the men were away the women would **brede** [make] the nets, when they came home they'd fit them out and they'd beet [mend] them. The women made our oilskin clothes by hand. They'd treat them with three coats of oil outside and one inside. New oilskin clothes were made every year and the women knitted the jerseys on eight steel needles.

'The fishing was good then. It was good until they found the herrings' spawning ground. What destroyed the shoals of herring was when the big boats discovered those grounds and the trawlers just went out there and let down their trawls — every year, you see, the herring would go back out there to spawn — and the trawlers would go there and just trawl them up. They'd come in, those boats, with the spawn actually spilling out over the side decks and that spoiled the herring fishing right down as far as Plymouth.

'The boy did all the jobs, pot scrubbing, deck scrubbing, coiling — when they shot the nets the boy would be down below coiling the rope around. During the day he'd be the cook and he'd also trim the lights, riding lights and steaming lamps, and make the tea. You had to work all the time, there was no rest.

'On Saturdays a couple of chaps'd go ashore with a cran basket vittling up for the week, steak and onions for Saturday night, roast beef for Sunday dinner, stew for Monday and three pieces of boiling beef to make broth. You'd make duff too in them days, you'd cook it in a condensed milk tin washed out and you'd make one for each of the men.

'When they'd all had their dinner you'd go up and wash all the plates and dishes on deck in the cold — and the saucepans. There was never much time to spare on the east coast, Plymouth was better.

'After sail we had steam. I was on a boat called the *Larkspur*, a mackerel boat. I remember once when the weather was very bad we were the only boat to stay out. We were fishing the mackerel off Cornwall then. I had to watch the line go overboard from the warp room below deck and make sure it didn't foul on anything. When half of it was gone, a huge wave struck the boat. I didn't know what happened. When I crawled up the water was all over the floorboards and the steam boiler had been put out. All hands had to get to the pumps to get the water out so we could relight the fires. When we got in my mother said, "you shall never go to sea again." It was so late when we got back with the boat everyone thought she'd gone.

'Then we got our own boat. Dad bought her just before the First World War. It was a family, six-handed boat and we had an engine put in and my next brother then had to take on learning to drive the engine. He only did one pilchard season before he was called up. All the boys, come 18, would join the Royal Naval Reserve – every little helped in those days and you did one month's drill every winter which fitted in a gap in the fishing when it was bad and you got a thirty bob retainer every quarter which paid the rent in those days. So everybody joined. Of course, come the war, they were the first ones to be called up.

'After the Plymouth fishing, you'd come home and take out the herring nets and put them in the loft and start the mackerel season. It was drifting them out of Mousehole and Newlyn then come July the mackerel nets would go into store, the big boats would be laid up and the smaller boats fitted out for pilchards.

'Of course the pilchards are long gone, but even I can remember the days when you'd pick up 50,000 pilchards at a shot – they'd be landed and pulled up to the pilchard stores with the big tanks in them where they'd be put in brine and after some weeks, taken out and washed and the women packed them in barrels. The oil was pressed out of them and then the pilchards were shipped mostly to Italy – a lot went to Leghorn. They were packed very pretty, like a rosette, with all the tails in the middle.

'They'd a rhyme about the pilchards and Italy:

"Here's health to the Pope may he live to repent,
And add half a year to the time of his Lent,
To teach all his children from Rome to the Poles,
There's nothing like pilchards for saving their souls."

My mother was a packer. Then suddenly the Italians didn't want the pilchards any more — perhaps they liked bananas better or something. But it would have been all the same, the shoals went.

'When we fished for mackerel we used the long line, 4000 hooks 11" apart. We used to do two trips a week from Newlyn, 85 to 90 miles off. We'd come in and land on a Wednesday and then go back out Thursday for a second trip.'

As I said in the introduction, Sunday fishing was a sore point with the Cornish but there were occasions. . . .

'Yes, I admit, I have been to sea on a Sunday but I never went unless I was forced to, not if I got a week's work proper, I'd be glad of a rest. But if not I'd think of the missus and the kids back home and see the bare cupboard and I'd go of a Saturday and Sunday. But only when I really had to.

'The first time I did it we were fishing for herring off Plymouth. We'd got nothing all week, no herring at all and things were looking pretty shy for Christmas. Then one little boat came in with a couple of cran on Friday night and I took it to be an omen. It was one week off Christmas — shall we go out, I thought?

'The men were agreeable so we went out on Saturday and early Sunday morning we'd a good shot. We landed them off the Barbican as the Salvation Army band was playing behind us — it was lovely. Then we went up to Sutton harbour to moor up with the old Cornish fleet and they said, "there's no place for you up here — go away and tie up with the Lowestoft boats." That night I went to the Wesley Chapel to be thankful we was blessed that Saturday night. There was bad weather after that all week so I picked up my £100 from the sales manager and got the train home and we all had a good Christmas. How the rest of the fleet got on I don't know, very bleak I'd think.'

Nettie, Jack's wife, died a little while ago. She gave these reminiscences at the age of 76 in 1976.

Fishing

'In bygone days superstition was rife. Women were not supposed to go on the piers and it was considered to be poor luck if a woman walked over a net which was about to be put on a boat. This signified that the net would surely be lost. One had to be careful what was said or done on the boat. No one dare mention rabbits or, for that matter, any four-legged animal. This was especially difficult for the young boys whilst sailing along the coast as many rabbits could be seen in the little meadows along the shore. I believe it was the same for miners going to Bal.

'Whistling was also taboo. Fishermen were careful what food they carried out to sea. Bread must be cut a certain way. Pasties were called "wind bags"; men said if they took a pasty they would be shut in Scilly for a week because of either a gale of wind or a calm. If one mentioned a preacher then it would be just as well to stay in as go to sea.

'When I was young I was very interested in hearing my father talk about these places [Ireland, Scotland, Scarborough, Whitby, etc.] and saying that when going up through the Caledonian Canal the children on the banks would shout out to them, "Hey, man, throw us out a bickey; hey, man throw us out a bickey." The fishermen, when they went on a long voyage, would carry sacks of hard biscuits with them.

'One hundred and fifty years ago fishermen would go to sea in the pilchard season and in fine weather, wearing bell-top hats, which were shorter than in later years and were very fashionable. Men also wore in the boats oilskin breeches and skirts. In my remembrance fishermen wore white barragon trousers, white duck frocks and carried their food in white, unbleached bags, and the womenfolk vied with one another as to who could scrub their men's clothes the whitest. The clothes would be taken in large zinc baths up under the shoot and streamed, no matter what the weather. I can never understand why fishermen wore white on their boats to do such dirty work.

'My mother told me about the capes fishermen used to wear. Before the boats were decked the men had no proper place to sleep, only under sails; in the night all the fishermen would wear large capes made of thick material called cape cloth, with hoods. When the boats came home from Plymouth after Christmas, the young men would go out when it was dark, wearing their dark, thick capes and if they met any young women, the men would take them up and drop them in a river. There were so many little rivers in the village. Of course, the rivers were not very deep so the young women could easily get out, but it was not a very pleasant experience. My mother told me that she had been taken up twice by young men and dropped in different rivers. Young women were afraid to go out alone in the nights, being afraid of "the capes".

'In our young days the harbour was a lovely sight, full of boats and with their sails hanging up to dry if they had been out in rough weather, the sails being of various shades, some patched with sailcloth of contrasting colour. We couldn't see the quays for the three tiers of boats — small pilchard drifters in under the wharf, larger boats in the middle tier and the largest boats by the quay. In the pilchard season when the pilchard fleet went out to sea it was a beautiful sight especially at night when the boats' lights were lit; the bay was lit up like a town.

'It was a thrilling sight during the pilchard season, from about the middle of June to the end of October, to see the pilchard boats going to sea in the afternoon and then to be on the quay from eight to ten o'clock and watch them come into the harbour, the fish shining like silver in the nets and the nets reeked half way up the mast. If our father's boat had a good catch we would run home as fast as our legs would carry us to tell our mother the good news. On other nights there would be no fish and we had no need to be told this when we saw that the hatches were laid.

'A "hatch" is a wood cover laid over the net hold. If the boats were late coming in and we had to go home to bed, we would know early in the morning if there had been any fish by the sound of horses and carts going through the village taking fish to the fish cellars to be cured with coarse salt in large tanks. I remember eight fish cellars here in our village which supplied quite a lot of work for men and women for about two or three months each year. Before the first war the wage paid to the workers in the cellars was three halfpence an hour during their first season and threepence an hour in subsequent seasons.

'If it came to thick fog after the pilchard drifters had gone to sea and the time was up for them to come back to harbour, I would go down to the old pier with my mother to rattle the large iron moorings rings that were on the head of the old pier. We would find other people there and they would take turns to rattle the rings. There was no foghorn in those days and the fishermen would hear the clink of the irons and know their whereabouts.

Village Life

'In my young days marinated pilchard was a tit-bit of our diet. Nearly all the fishermen's wives would have a pan of fish marinated every week and they were delicious.

'There were always two or three women in the village who marinated pilchards for sale, but nowadays we rarely see pilchards. The fisherfolk always had "bussas" of fish salted down for use in winter. There would also be dried salt hake and cod. Unlike now, the children did not play on the rocks around Carn Topna as the fishermen always put their hake and cod out there to dry on the flat rocks when the tide was out. Also the women who lived nearby would dry their clothes on the rocks, stones being put on sheets and table cloths to keep them down.

'In walking through the village one would also see fish hanging by string from nails on the walls of houses until they were as dry as chips; they would then be wrapped in paper and put away until winter. When the boats came home from Ireland the men would bring hundredweights of potatoes with them; they could buy them more cheaply in Ireland than back home.

'Fishermen's wives had to be very thrifty as there was no unemployment benefit in those days. The long winter was a terrifying time to look forward to and so the woman of the house would take the precaution of having a large sack of flour, one or two "bussas" of butter salted in, eggs pickled and dried fish. The wife could then rest assured that they were prepared for any emergency and would be happy to see the barrels of fish in the cellar and sacks and pans of food in the pantry. I look back on those dear people as people of great courage, never knowing from one day to another if their husbands would get a shilling.

'Up to forty years ago there were few visitors. The village was without sanitation, lights or piped water. Water had to be carried in pails and pitchers. We carried ours from Pedna-caunse, a small stream brought through a pipe in Raginnis Hill. In the summertime one would have to wait for a dozen or more people to fill their pitchers owing to the smallness of the stream. There was a second stream of drinking water at Coronation Place, a third at the shoot in Paul Lane, and a fourth at Fox's Lane. There was a shoot near Warren's Cafe in Chapel Street, but the water was unfit for drinking. We would go to that shoot on Mondays for clothes-washing water. Washing in those days was hard work, one had to bring in all the water and very often this was the woman's job, the men having gone to sea. Water was boiled on a flip [an open fire with a boiler on top] in the cellar, or on the slab [kitchen range] as the case may be.

'Ironing was done with a box and heater. One had to keep in a very bright fire to get the iron heater red-hot and as one was taken out of the fire, another one was put in. As the heaters were smaller they would rattle in the box and sometimes make a mess on the article being ironed because of the "blacks" [coal dust] coming out.

'Then there was the old-fashioned box mangle which we used before the smaller mangle was invented. I enjoyed going with my mother to a house with a large cellar adjoining. This cellar had cobble stones on the ground and contained a large box mangle. The top of the mangle was a great wooden box containing rocks for weight. This was on smooth wooden rollers around which the clothes were wrapped and rolled. It would mangle the clothes beautifully and I only wish I could explain it more distinctly.

'Water, sanitation and electric light came at about the same time, 1924. This meant much less work, no oiling of lamps or trimming of wicks and cleaning the chimneys of the lamps. Most people had white calico blinds at their windows and the light would shine out into the roads. There were no street lights. How our ancestors would enjoy the amenities of today! Another blessing is the electric cooker. Until thirty or forty years ago there were in the village six public bake-houses to which people took their dinner, puddings, pies and cakes to be baked. All knew their own dishes, each family having its own special mark — we baked our food in the Keigwin bake-house. We baked bread twice a week or more and at Christmas the black cakes that women made were put in the ovens at 6 p.m. and everything else was taken out.

'My early remembrances are all of sounds. The hokey-pokey man selling ice cream was an Italian. He had a donkey to pull a little cart and would shout, "Hokey-pokey, penny a lump; the more you have the more you want." Ice cream was not put in biscuits then but wrapped in greaseproof paper.

'The sixpenny-ha'penny bazaar came every month with its wares; it consisted of a long waggon with buckets, saucepans, baskets, frying pans, etc. all hanging around the waggon, jingling and jangling with the movement of the horse pulling it along. Cups and saucers, all and sundry, and everything for sixpence-ha'penny, hardly believable today. The women would be running to it from all directions.

'In the fruit season you would hear the men shouting, "Apples, apples, 3d. a pottle, 6d. a gallon, oranges four or six a penny". The vegetable man came every day crying out, "Taties, taties, turnips, cabbages". The fisherman or "jowster" as we called him, driving his pony, would be shouting, "pilchards, six a penny", or mackerel or herring as the case may be, "four a penny". You would see women running out with their plates.

'Once in a while a man driving a donkey and cart would come from Penzance ringing a bell and shouting, "iron, iron, any old iron?" On Fridays a man would come from Perranuthnoe selling sand. He would shout, "sand, sand, halfpenny a bucket, halfpenny a bucket", the pail in which he measured the sand hanging from the back of his cart. Some of the cottages had stone floors and the women liked to sprinkle sand around the fireplace. I would also like to mention Charlie, who went through the village ringing his bell, calling out the events of the week.'

Joe Tonkin provides a postscript to the Penders' accounts. He spends his retirement days in the Seaman's Mission on the old quay at Newlyn, the bigger fishing port which lies between Mousehole and Penzance where the Great Newlyn Fishing Battle was fought, which is described in Chapter 7.

The mission is a fine place where the old can sit and reminisce and where those still working in the industry, both native Cornish and from ports all over Europe, can come in for a shower, a warm-up and some hot food day or night. The young fishermen play pool as they wait for the weather to change, the old tell of past storms, of mighty catches and of the 'great old days' of the fishing.

'The windows look out over the harbour so that the boats can be seen coming and going, the size of the catch estimated at a distance by the retired fishermen by how low she is in the water. In heavy weather the sea chases up the river which lies at the back of the mission, behind a huge granite wall, and punches like a battering ram.

'I first went to sea at 14 on a big mackerel boat. They'd just gone on to engines then but they'd still got one big sail, the engines weren't powerful enough. Those old men were hard, really hard, there wasn't no rest for a boy then. It didn't matter if you were sick nor sorry, you worked just the same. Later, when I had boys on my own boat I tried to remember what it had been like and be a bit better with them.

'When I started I did all the cooking, going ashore when we put in to do the shopping. It was mainly barley broth with beef — in them days beef, especially brisket, was a cheap meat. You cleaned and scrubbed, work down below, you never stopped.

'In my father's time there were hundreds and hundreds of boats in Newlyn, but very different boats than there are today. The fishing was different, too. I've been up fishing off Plymouth when there's been over a hundred Cornish boats and another hundred from Lowestoft and enough herring for everyone. That was before they all got greedy. You'd go for

two or three months around Christmas time and there'd be
tens of thousands of fish and some mackerel and pilchards too.
Yet you had to be tough.

'They used to be very religious here, you know. They didn't
do nothing on a Sunday and they certainly didn't fish. Then
the Lowestoft boys would come down and they'd fish and
there'd be some old fights. The Newlyn boys would chuck the
Lowestoft boys' fish back in the harbour. In my father's time
they had to bring in a regiment of troops after one big battle, to
stop them. I remember as a lad catching a few fish on a line
one Sunday and we were very short at the time. My mother
never said nothing but I knew what she thought and when I
fried them up she wouldn't eat them.

'As a boy on a boat you'd work for a share like all the rest,
but being a boy it was a very small one. You wouldn't get them
working for that kind of money today. They were usually
family boats. John Jack Pender had five brothers and a cousin
on his. In our family my father and brother and a brother-in-
law and two nephews all had a boat together, and so on.
They'd call the boats then after someone in the family. Ours
was the *Lizzie Tonkin*, then we got one called *Mary Jane*. They
go in for flashier names nowadays.

'But they've gone mad now, quite mad. They spent all those
millions on the new quay and just look out there, look at all
those big, expensive boats tied up and yet the weather good
. . . no fish. First they overfished the pilchards, then the
herrings – the German boats, trawlers as big as the Icelandic
ones, came down to Plymouth and destroyed the herring, then
the mackerel. Everyone told the Government you couldn't
keep taking mackerel like that, the big trawlers and the factory
ships and so on, but they kept saying their scientists said there
was plenty out there. Then they'd all that money invested in
new boats and big new gear and they'd plans for the new quay
for years and no one would stop them building it and now what?

'After the pilchards they thought it didn't matter as there
was herring and when the herring was all gone there was still
the mackerel. I suppose they think that after the mackerel
there'll be something else but if there is, I don't know what it
is. It's live for today or at the most the week, with no thought
for the future.

'Yet there was *so much* mackerel. You'd go out fishing then
from Monday to Friday and expect to be away a week. On the
herring you'd be away two to three months, getting home only
for weekends or Christmas Day. Of course the weather could
really hold you up then. We used to go up off Cardiff mackerel
fishing and you'd set off and be caught in bad weather and
have to tie up in the Scillies for a week or more. You'd be there
earning nothing and there was nothing you could do about it.
Times are not so hard now. The young lads just go and sign on
when there's no fishing. It certainly wasn't like that before,
you'd go out in all weathers unless it was really impossible
because you had to. If there was no fish there was no money.

'If the old people came back now they wouldn't recognise
Newlyn apart from the old quay. There was no houses up the
hill, no council estates, no bungalows, just two separate parts
of the town with families living in the houses they'd been in
for generations. There was trouble way back even when they
wanted to join the two halves of the town with a road, the tide
used to separate them then. Now the cottages are second
homes, holiday homes and so on and the young fishermen live
in council houses when they can get them or move away.

'Those of us who remember sit in the Seamen's Mission and
talk over old times. It's a grand old place. They let all the old
boys in here, even if they've not been fishermen, which I think
is nice since it's warm and comfortable. I don't suppose you
get that kind of thing in England. . . .'

7

The Great Newlyn Fishing Battle

Fishermen everywhere, as well as being brave and hardy, are superstitious and were deeply religious. The Cornish fishermen, as John Jack Pender and Joe Tonkin have said, were against fishing on a Sunday. Most of them were Wesleyans and any kind of activity on the Sabbath was strictly prohibited. Even I can dimly remember visiting relatives who went in for the Cornish Sunday even in the late 1940s. Sewing would be left on the machine, washing left unironed, even the radio was never switched on. Chapel going was the order of the day and obviously fishing was virtually unheard of.

However in the spring, when the boats from Yarmouth and Lowestoft came down to west Cornwall, their fishermen had no such inhibitions. Human nature, though, is human nature. A week of bad weather and no fish would be followed by a glorious Saturday night and Sunday morning and the Cornishmen would have to stand on the quays and watch the East Anglians setting off to fish, then returning laden with a huge catch. Anger and envy, mixed with religion, is a strong and heady brew.

For several years at the end of the last century, trouble simmered on the quays, with the Cornish finally trying to prevent the fish going off to market, and there was an increasing number of fights. Matters became even worse when a small number of Cornish fishermen also decided to fish on

Sunday evenings, causing even more trouble.

It all came to a head in May of 1896 with what came to be
described as the Great Newlyn Fishing Battle in which the
fathers of John Jack Pender and Joe Tonkin took part. On
Sunday 17 May 'persuasion', in the form of punch-ups and
arguments, failed to stop the Lowestoft men putting out to sea
and when they returned to Newlyn Harbour, the locals raided
the boats and threw the fish into the harbour. Some 100,000
fish ended up in the sea and fights broke out.

On the following Tuesday morning six more Lowestoft boats
arrived in Newlyn to be greeted by an angry crowd which
promptly threw their catches overboard. By the afternoon the
police were desperately trying to keep the two warring factions
apart while supporters from other fishing villages began to
arrive in force to join in on the side of the Newlyn men. In
desperation the authorities telegraphed to the Government
asking for gunboats and troops. It gave the local *Cornish
Telegraph* the story of the editor's dreams.

By Friday, three hundred soldiers from the Second Berkshire
Regiment had arrived in Cornwall, under the command of a
Major Hassard. They marched to Newlyn quay from Penzance
railway station where they were welcomed by the local
population with jeers and catcalls. Six magistrates strode out
bravely at their head. The troops took possession of the south
pier, just as a torpedo boat destroyer, the *Ferret*, arrived in
Mount's Bay. Fighting really got under way then in earnest.
Some Cornishmen continued to fight with the East Anglians;
others joined forces with them to attack the troops. According
to local legend, the entire St Ives and Porthleven fishing fleets
sailed into Newlyn harbour with flags flying to fight off the
English army. At this point a contingent of Penzance fishermen
arrived to fight on the side of the Lowestoft men, rivalry
between Penzance and Newlyn having been ferocious for
years.

The soldiers fired volleys over the incoming boats, huge
battles were fought up and down the quays and the beleag-
uered local authorities requested yet more help which came in
the form of the ships HMS *Curlew* and HMS *Traveller* (both
carrying armed seamen), later joined by HMS *Leda*. By this
time Whitehall was becoming concerned over the ability of a

group of fishermen to tie up three hundred soldiers and four warships.

Gradually tempers abated. The St Ives and Porthleven boats returned home, and the Lowestoft men moored in Penzance Harbour where the inhabitants were more sympathetic. Most of the regiment was sent home and £800 damages were paid to the Lowestoft Boat Owners' Association.

Trouble on a smaller scale flickered around the coast in subsequent years, but never again on such a grand scale. What the story — amusing as it is nearly a hundred years on — does show was the sheer size of the industry at the turn of the century. What was not in doubt was that there was sufficient fish for all.

8

The silver darlings

Herring fishing from Yarmouth and Lowestoft

While Newlyn's silver harvest was pilchards, in East Anglia it was herring. Yarmouth port goes back to A.D. 1000 when a number of houses were built on land 'which had come out of the sea'. The port would appear never to have looked back.

Some two hundred years ago there were many fishing craft off the town called 'herring buses', and according to Charles Temple, who has recorded much of the town's history, in 1751 there were 250 Dutch 'buses', each with a crew of fourteen which caught an average of 20 lasts each — a last being 13,000 fish; 120 Schevelling boats of 30 tons, 120 French buses of 100 tons with crews of between fifteen and twenty-five which could catch 3000 lasts of fish, apart from the local fleets. In 1853 the Yarmouth boats alone caught 10,000 lasts of herring.

He says,

'at first there were the buses, then came the luggers, so called because they had three irregular square or lug sails and were noted for their swiftness. Eventually steam became the driving force: at first very unpopular, because of frequent breakdowns, but in time, with more powerful engines, the steam vessels fished alongside the sailing craft and gradually replaced them at the end of the last century.'

George Crisp spent his life on the land but he came from a family of fishermen.

'My dad he was a fisherman out of Lowestoft. He lived down near the Duke of York in Ditchingham all his life and he died at 92. He left home when he was 11 years old. Never, never had no good home life so one day he decided he'd had enough and off he went one early morning.

'Now there used to be trains in those days running from Ditchingham to Lowestoft but my Dad he hadn't got enough money to go all that way so he walked down to Beccles to catch a train from there. Someone told his mother later on that they'd a-seen him walking off all along the road with a pillow-case slung over his shoulder. Only 11 years old, think of that.

'When he got down to Lowestoft he got a berth on a boat as a cook. That was how the little old boys started in those days. Dad started in the sailing days, of course. He used to say that the old sailing fishing boats were a lot better financially than the steam drifters as he said the money went out of the old funnels from the steam drifter but the wind was always free.

'He was real tough, Dad. When you think of him going off on the boat at the age he was and it was really hard. You used to sleep on an old straw bed at night and you'd work all day. He was always a crew man. My uncles now, they were skippers out of Lowestoft but not Dad. My mother used to make all his jumpers [smocks] for him. I used to get the calico for her and then she'd buy this special kind of pitch and tan them. They used to do this so they would be waterproof. She'd do the old man's jumpers in a big bowl, boiling them up on the kitchen range. Do you know why they were made like that with no buttons? So that when they were hauling in the nets they'd not catch. If there'd have been buttons on they'd a-caught in the nets as they come in. That was their uniform, them jumpers. The old chaps'd wear them all their life because they were so warm.

'My mother was never happy about him being at sea. Mind you, she'd a hard time of it too, there was nine of us. When the weather was bad and stormy you could hear her walking the bedroom floor, up and down, up and down, worrying about the storm. At one time she persuaded him to give it up

and he took on a milk round. He used to go out early and buy
the milk and then hawk it around Bungay. Well there were
these two fishermen, old Gunner and old Samson, and they
were laying down drunk in the churchyard. There'd been
snow all night and my father was driving his milk cart along
when he saw these two little old boys laying on this stone heap
in the churchyard. So he went across to them and he said to
one of them, "Come you on now George, what the hell are you
doing laying out here like this in the churchyard", and old
George he answered, "there's one thing about this place, the
landlord do have put on some lovely white sheets." There he
was, covered in snow, with only his face sticking out. These
two old boys had got drunk in the town and tried to walk
home and that was as far as they could get.

'But my Dad went on back to the fishing. He'd the sea right
in his blood by then. He was never seasick nor nothing.
During the 1914-18 war he done the turn for the blokes taking
the soldiers over on the boat as they was all took so bad they
couldn't do their shift.

'He could put up with a lot. He'd come home with his hands
very sore. The jumpers would rub on his wrists and then when
he hauled in the nets they'd sometimes bring them up full of
nettle fish, stinging fish he used to call them and his hands'd
be full of stings. What tough little old boys they were.

'But the pay was good. In those days it was the best work
around here in East Anglia, otherwise it was all work on the
land. That was in the sailing and the steam days, the herring
and the deep sea fishing. My uncles and my dad earned good
money although you took your risk. Uncle Vic was the skipper
of a boat when he got washed over the taffrail and drowned
while my other uncle was working on the same boat. Another
brother he worked in a printing works at Bungay but when his
brother came home and chucked his golden sovereigns on the
table and he saw he'd been paid 20 or 30 gold sovereigns, then
he said no more printing works for me and he was off down
after the fishing too, taking the dead brother's place.

'When they come home from the sea and what they call
"made up", that is got their pay, then they used to go into the
watch house and be drinking beer all day, all day on the juice
they'd be.

'I remember one old bloke named Beckham. He lived in Bridge Street, Bungay and he was an old character, a proper old fisherman at the same time as my father. There was no end to the tales about him. One night he come home from the fishing and his wife had a bowl of starch on the table — in those days they used to make it overnight for the washing. Well when he got in he looked on the table and said, "is that all you can do while I'm away and all I can come back to — some old arrowroot?" and he didn't wait to hear what she said but got it all into him and after he said he was that stiff he couldn't go upstairs. . . .

'Years later when he was an old man, living by himself, he went up Bridge Street hill shouting out "fire, fire". It was a right bitter winter. Someone asked him, "where's the fire, Mr Beckham?" and he said "in everybody's bloody house bar mine".

'My Dad went to sea until he was nearly 70 and would have gone on past that if they'd let him. He never had a day off work. My uncles were the same. When one of them retired at 81, he used to make and mend nets down in Lowestoft. He used to have an old shed and he'd be in there working away with all those nets hanging up around him. You see, they didn't know what it was to retire.'

One thing which seems common to both Newlyn and Lowestoft fishermen was the type of food they ate. As well as fish, of course, and boiled beef, they all seemed to eat duff. A recipe for the duff made on one Lowestoft drifter describes how eggs were used in the mixture. The suet came directly from the butcher and it had to be grated, not cut. It could then be flavoured later as desired and was eaten either as a savoury, with meat or gravy, or with treacle, jam or rhubarb. The boy cook was not allowed to cut it to see if were properly done, he had to prick it lightly with a fork to see if it glistened. All this, of course, had to be done in appalling cramped surroundings, very often in extremely rough weather and with no proper facilities.

Frank Fisk, an old Lowestoft fisherman in his seventies, remembers,

'You had no facilities. There weren't no toilets in them days neither, only a round tub which you all had to use. If you wanted to go ashore when you were away on voyage, you all had to wait for each other till you'd done washing in the buckets, in the pails. When you went to bed you lay on a bag of straw. Yes, that you did. When I went away on a voyage I used to have to go to a farmer and get some straw and make a bed from it. There were bunks in the cabins and you used to put a straw bed in and lay on that. You never took your clothes off. I used to turn in just as I am now.

'You always eat well on the boats. The stoker used to clean all the fish for breakfast, all the herring, and he used to wash them in a pail. The cook used to fry them up. You always used pails for different jobs because there wasn't nothing else. If you wanted to get some water over the side of the boat you used a bucket with a rope on but you'd never twist that rope round your hand because if you did that it might pull you over. You used to have it so if that did try to take you over you could let go. Sometimes when there was a bit of a breeze, a man would get knocked overboard. That used to happen on the cast off sometimes when he was taking the seizins off the rope. The rope would jump out of the mole-jenny [fair lead] and knock him over the side. There bin many a man lost that way, specially if there was a bit of a swell on.

'I mean, you went to sea in all weathers. Oh, that'd got to blow hellish hard to stop you from going out. Sometimes that'd be mountains high. When you went round t'Westward that was like that. When we went round t'Newlyn the sea would go right up high. Well of course you'd go up with it and then you'd come down. Sometimes you used to wonder just where you were going. You always kept the boat into the wind. That'd knock along for evermore if you kept into the wind with the sail up. We used to be out for a week at a time in bad weather, and we didn't fish at all because it was too rough. All you did was keep dodgin'. You put your mizzen sail up, set that dead in the middle and then you went into the wheelhouse and set the wheel. She used t'be so steady that you could go t'sleep and let her dodge along. The only thing you mustn't do was let her go off across the wind or else you would have a bit of a flap on.

'I can describe when we were round there once at Newlyn and we all had to come in because of the weather. That was as fine as silk at dinner-time, about twelve or one o'clock time, and then that come on a gale about two. We had t'batten down. We battened down everywhere and then all the wheelhouse windows got knocked out. We managed to get into Newlyn all right, but nearly every drifter lost a mizzen mast or a little boat or something. That was a proper rough day that was. One of the boats — it might've been the *Welcome Friend* — actually lost her wheelhouse. That was washed away by the sea and she hadn't got nothing, only a plain deck. Her mast was gone as well and the bulwarks were all broke. I don't know how she managed to get into Newlyn, but there was a crowd of people t'see her come in. Yes, we used t'get some rough weather round there — off the Bishop Rock and down the Lizard and the Longships. That was marvellous how them little old drifters used to stick it.

'When we went away we all used to have a little ditty-box to keep medicines in and writing paper and what little money you had . . . just a little wooden box. I used to bring mine home at the end of the voyage. You used to have embrocations and things like that in it. Mrs Love's Ointment as well. We used to take that for the hands. Up at Shields you used to get these jellyfish. Cor, they were murder! They used to sting you and I've known blokes t'put reed bags over their heads and cut holes in for the eyes when they were hauling up the nets. They did that 'cos the jellies stung so. After you'd done hauling you used t'wash in the warm water that came out of the engine room.'

9

Mending the nets

Jessie Thacker

Nobody could call Lowestoft a beautiful town, not even the holidaymakers who clutter up the streets during the summer. It is what it has always been, a practical fishing port, a workmanlike place where trawlers lie four deep along the harbour wall and where the smell of wet fish hangs heavy in the air. Like the ports of the west country, those of East Anglia have also felt the pinch as fishing grounds become restricted, and fish stocks fall off.

Like the west country fishermen they have fished the herring and the mackerel but they have also had a large proportion of deep sea boats, going out after white fish.

Up in J. and W. Stuart's big loft, the women make the trawl nets. Lacy clouds of net hang on rods while the women's hands, with the shuttles, move back and forth so quickly you can't even see them. In this machine conveyor-belt age it is remarkable that something as big as a trawl net, averaging 80 feet by 84, is still made by hand, every loop of it. But it is very fast dying out as the ubiquitous machines take over.

Jessie Thacker has been making nets for fifty years.

'But then there'd have been eighty women working here, not eight. But you can't get the girls to go in for it. They do their

training and then off they go to Bird's Eye where they can
shovel peas down a chute for twice as much. It'll have to be
done by machine in the end, the machines will take over.

'Why aren't they all made by machine yet? Well, because a
trawl isn't just a simple thing. It's as difficult as a knitting
pattern, made up of large pattern pieces which all have to be
shaped and no machine so far has been made that can produce
anything but straight lengths.'

Jessie began making nets in the days when the Lowestoft
fishermen went after the herrings but this had already begun
to tail off at the end of the war and the herring fishing has now
virtually ceased. With them, the herrings have taken away a
whole way of life in this part of Suffolk: it has completely
disappeared.

'In those days the women used to come down from Scotland
following the herring. They'd gut and clean the fish, wearing
old oilies and boots, with black Shetland scarves around their
heads and their fingers all tied up with rags because they kept
cutting them on fish bones. Old grannies would come, young
girls, married women, all sorts: they'd start off in the Shetlands
at Lerwick and they'd go down the coast of Scotland, then to
Shields and Grimsby, Yarmouth and they'd get here about the
first week in September.

'Work – you've never seen anyone work so hard. Excepting
on Sunday, they wouldn't work then nor the fishing fleet (the
Scots boys that is), you know how religious Scottish people are
about Sundays. Local folk used to clear out their two front
downstairs rooms, even taking up the lino, and leave them a
table and a bed and then rent it out to the fish women. They'd
take about four girls who each paid 4s. a week which was
reasonable money in those days. Each girl would bring a huge
trunk with her in which she kept all her things and then she'd
use it as a seat and you'd know when the girls were there
because you saw the oilies in the front gardens.

'Of course, on a Sunday, there was a houseful of all the
relations who were in the fleet or at least they'd *say* they were
entertaining their relations. And they were the most marvellous knitters. They'd knit in Fair Isle, in complicated Arran

patterns, always in dark blue. Their men called the jerseys their "go ashores" meaning their best ones and while they'd buy jerseys for working, they'd always have handknitted "go ashores" for walking out. But those houses used to stink, they smelt of oil and fish gut so no wonder they used to clear the places out when they came.

'When they went out at night, the girls never went out on their own, they always went five or six abreast, in a clan, perhaps because they thought there was safety in numbers. "Scottish muggies", the local people called them. I don't know why. In a good season they'd earn perhaps £20 for four months' work.'

Jessie was one of a family of eleven children,

'but my mother also brought up a young brother and sister and the child of one of my sisters, so that made fourteen at table. Father earned £1 a week at the gasworks and 5s. for working overtime. Each week he spent the 5s. on leather and he'd inspect our shoes to see whose had to be repaired.

'We weren't allowed to talk at table, we had to get on with our food − not that there was much of it to get on with. Father played the trombone and was very musical. Every Sunday night he'd make us sing and it was agony for one of my sisters because she couldn't sing a note in tune. Father said *everybody* could sing, and used to walk around with his ear near our mouths making sure we were.'

Like many old people, however, she feels her early life must have been hard, but it was good.

'They were grand days, though. I wouldn't have missed them for anything although it was a plain way of life, even things like apples and oranges and jellies you only saw at Christmas.

'As each girl got to 13, she went out to work as a netmaker or braider. My eldest sister got 2s. 6d. a week when she started and for that she had to make two nets. They were smaller then, of course, they were small mesh ones for the sailing smacks but it was still a lot of work. It had gone up a bit when

I started but not all that much. We didn't have this lovely soft
Terylene string then, it was all tarred string. It used to cut your
hands to ribbons, to shreds. The netmakers used to be laid up
for a couple of months in the summer while the fleet was away
and our hands would be all soft and ladylike from washing up
in a boarding house or something, then when we came back to
braiding, we'd end up with our hands covered in rags.

'There weren't no plasters then so you had to use bandages.
There were old fashioned remedies about then for curing the
cuts, like rubbing paraffin in and . . . no, I can't tell you, it's
too disgusting. Old wives' tales, I supposed, but the paraffin
helped and so did the one I daren't tell you about.'

She was very reticent about this but I gathered the base
material of the mix was urine.

'Nowadays in the spring, we use a harsher green twine
because it doesn't catch on the bottom and is at its worst in
spring, and then our hands get a bit sore as it is so much stiffer
but it's not as bad as it was years ago. We start to make the
green nets about February.

'Another old skill was beasting. The beasters used to repair
the nets. They'd get 5s. a week and 1s. for each net they'd
repaired and sometimes the whole bottom was out of a net and
it was an enormous job.

'Now we're paid on a day rate. It helps the slow ones
because they were only taking home about £5 a week until as
recently as the mid-1960s. The nets aren't made all the same,
you know. Many are tailored to fit the individual requirements
of the trawler skippers. They'll come along and tell us their
ideas and how they'd like the nets to be made and we make it
up for them. They're very much the same now because I think
the present day trawls are as good as anyone can get, they
don't need much alteration. Then the trawler owners get
together too and discuss the best patterns for nets — they meet
here and, you know, wheels within wheels and the devil turns
the handle. . . .'

Jessie married a trawlerman, now retired, and has twin sons
who are marine engineers. 'Guess what their hobby is —

fishing! When I've spent all day in here making nets, I go home to find nets on the lawn that they want mended and the whole family running in and out worrying about the wind.'

When they got the chance trawlers could make £8000 on a trip in the mid-seventies ranging across the Atlantic and bringing home tons of cod and flatfish, but the fleet has dwindled considerably even since then. Jessie remembers the days of the herring with true pleasure.

'I saw that telly film *Shoals of Herring* the other night and it wasn't really much like that. My husband says they don't know any more what a real shoal is. When they pulled in the nets in the film the herring in them were only a shimmer of herrings, nothing like a shoal. When they caught a real shoal, my husband would stand there up to his waist, up to his neck even, in herrings. A cran of herrings was four baskets and a good shoal would be 300 or so cran. I suppose in the last days of the herring, nobody wanted to take pictures so there is no record of it.

'The herring days were the happy ones, and my childhood. I lived in the beach village and the cox of the lifeboat was next door. Long ago, they'd no telephones or any way of telling people they were needed for the lifeboat so they'd send runners around the town banging on doors and crying, "they're running down, they're running down", and that's what I remember most vividly, the dark stormy night, the rain and those eerie voices shouting, "they're running down". Then we'd all go down to the beach and push the boat out.'

A lot of labour goes into those nets, the cod ends (the bag which holds the fishes whether cod or not), the great wings that help it slip through the water. Across from the Ladies' Room (as the loft is known where Jessie works), the men sew the pattern pieces together and the white lace and orange nets fill the space like a mad stage design. It will be sad when all the nets appear from the end of a large machine.

Says Jessie,

'You see, I'm so much better off than, say, the car workers. How many other people can look at a ball of string, start with that and end up with the finished product, the complete net? I'm responsible for it all the way through and those car workers can't say that, can they, however much they earn? And when one of our trawlers wins the port record for a catch, the men'll come over and say, "Thank you, Jessie".'

10

Oysters and crabs

Side by side with the major Cornish fishing industry, there has always existed a far more specialised branch of it — oyster dredging. Oyster fishermen are somewhat different even now, fishing in the traditional way they have for centuries and without the benefit of any modern technology. Theirs is a highly specialised kind of fishing but even for them, the problems besetting the fishing industry as a whole are staring them in the face.

Even the oysters are being overfished and the oystermen themselves have realised that unless drastic action is taken — by them — then the oyster will follow the mackerel and the pilchard into oblivion. The oystermen have taken their own stringent precautions therefore. Captain John Whitehouse, harbourmaster and water bailiff, tells the history of the free oyster fishery on the Fal, while Henry Merrifield speaks of a lifetime on the river.

But if ordinary fishing and oyster dredging are under threat, other kinds of shellfish sales are positively booming. Most fishermen and many people who lived along the coast kept a few lobsterpots for themselves and could make a few bob selling crabs and lobsters to boarding houses and hotels, but now crabs are big business as Jack Harvey of Newlyn describes. In fact the business is so big one can only speculate if the stocks of crabs can stand it.

What all three men admit is that there is still a lot about shellfish we don't know. There are gaps in our knowledge of the life cycles of lobsters and crayfish and as for oysters — as Henry Merrifield says, 'oysters is a mystery'.

Oysters is a mystery

Oysters were a delicacy to the Romans, a commonplace to the Victorians and are a luxury now. The free fishery on the Fal river dates back to Roman times. The Romans dredged there for oysters, the Phoenicians, trading in tin, bought them and took them away. Free oyster fisheries, that is those which are not privately owned, are now a real rarity.

Unhappily, after providing a secure living for centuries, even the great Fal oyster beds are now beginning to feel the effects of overfishing. From his cosy harbour office on the quay at Truro, where the Fal becomes a narrow, lazy river, Captain John White, Truro harbour master and water bailiff, described how the free fishery is organised. The upper reaches of the Fal are his territory, right down through the free fishery until it passes into the domain of the Falmouth harbour master. He is a vigorous man, always busy.

'The fishing is regulated by the Truro Port Fishery Order 1936, later amended by the Port Fishing Order (Open Variation) 1975 — I tell you this not to blind you with legalities but because it will assume some importance later on! The "free" area covers 2,271 acres of fishing beds (1,101 hectares in today's terms but nobody around here uses such a measurement) and the limit of it is from Malpas down a line from Castle Point to Trefusis Point. The extent of the fishery is all that water which lies within that boundary below mean low water mark — a large area.

'There were regulating orders before this century from the days when Truro City Council, as it then was, was the regulating authority. In the 1960s there was a move afoot to establish a "several" fishery, that's a fishery owned or operated by "a person or persons or company adjacent to the free fishery", but the fishermen decided they would fight this for reasons of their own; mainly they thought that if there was a "several" fishery adjoining the "free" fishery irregularities could easily take place. . . . The whole matter ended up with a huge row and a major public enquiry, followed by an appeal, but our fishermen won their case. They also had their boundary extended into the area which was to have been used by the several fishery so they came well out of it.

'If the situation was more hopeful this area could be cultivated and brought back into production — at the moment it's so heavily encrusted with weed, coral, and various things that this is not possible, but at least it provides a buffer against any encroachment to the free fishery.

'However as time went on many of the older rules and regulations got thrown out, although the main one was kept which is the size of the ring — oysters which are small enough to pass through the ring must be thrown back — and the time and manner in which oystermen are able to dredge.

'The fishery is still fished entirely in the traditional manner, that is under oars or sails, and in the new regulations it specifically states that dredging for oysters or mussels within the fishery must be undertaken only by vessels powered by sails or oars and such vessels may catch oysters by the dragging of an apparatus over the sea bed, such apparatus being capable of being hauled by hand or handwinch. The idea is that it is an inefficient way of fishing — you will appreciate that. If you were to take that area of fishery and dredge by power, you could put down lines in a close cross pattern and in no time you would clear the whole area. You could box the whole fishery up and clear it up but in reality, with sail boats going with wind and tide, they drag the dredge in one direction and then sail back in the other, so you can see from the pattern that they are missing oysters all the time so that at the end of the season there are oysters left to self-propagate.

'Having said that we are now going through a problem of overfishing. There are too many fishermen. It is a free fishery and that is the whole crux of the matter. Although it's not free in the sense of no cash passing hands, anybody can do it provided they obey the regulations and pay a licence fee. Literally anyone can go in there and fish.

'What has happened in the past is that the number of

fishermen fishing for oysters kept relatively stable but now it is going up and up. The oyster is a self-propagating mollusc and ours are not cultivated. Our oysters are a natural phenomenon and frankly there are too many people taking too many oysters. So what has happened now is that oysters have become relatively scarce, so much so that in November the fishermen held a meeting and decided that they would have a voluntary embargo on oyster fishing starting on 1 January 1982. This meant that although they had taken out a licence, the fishing was so bad they decided voluntarily not to fish for the rest of the season. We backed that up with a regulating order to see the cowboys didn't go in and fish when the good guys had given it up. If everybody around our coastline had done the same with the fishing that the Fal men have done we wouldn't be in the mess we are in today.

'I don't know if this will be a lasting solution but I think it's a step on the right road. I think, too, that the licence fee has been pitched at too low a level and although we can't regulate the numbers of people who go on the fishery — it's right that we shouldn't and that's what the free fishery is all about — we have to think about regulating the amount of oysters taken. Maybe it will come down to protecting the fishery by economic sanctions but that's a matter for the ministry.

'Nobody has ever made a fortune oyster fishing, but it's been marvellous steady work for a large number of families around the Fal, the sort of thing that is handed on from father to son. You see the boys who were school kids when I first came down here now having their own sail boats. It's a traditional thing, a traditional means of making a living which has virtually died out elsewhere.

'The oyster is very odd. It's a self-propagating hermaphrodite. In order for it to grow, the spat — which is the tiny little oyster — has to come down and settle and grow on another piece of oyster shell or a mussel or something. So what has happened in the past is that with constant dredging you tend to get large piles of this stuff in the fishery. What the fishermen are doing now is coming back to cultivate. They come with their dredges, but without the net so that nothing gets caught, and trail the knife behind the vessel to distribute the old shell in which the spat settles. So what the fisherman is doing by going over the fishery without catching anything is to drag the shell or culch down from the high water mark and spread it more evenly over the fishery to try and catch more spat in it. In addition there is the climate — there's no real scientific evidence for this, it's only a hypothesis, but you really need an ambient temperature of 16 degrees to get a good spat fall, so if you get a relatively cold summer, water-wise, then the oyster doesn't spat or if it does then not in prolific quantities.

'An oyster ring now is 2⅝" in diameter — we haven't gone metric. I felt it should have done when we went into hectares but the fishermen were determined to cling on to the old measurement. Why 2⅝"? Don't ask me. An oyster will be about 2½ years old by then.

'One of the real advantages of the Fal is that there is no disease here. French oyster beds are riddled with disease. We have the dreaded Japanese seaweed now but the main predators of the oyster are the slipper limpet and the tingle — rather romantic names for very unromantic creatures. The tingle is a little thing which clamps on to the oyster and bores its way through and either kills it directly or smothers it. Then there are starfish. Fishermen who are conservation-minded pick up slipper limpets, tingles and starfish and then put them on the beach to dry out. We do not allow any oysters from anywhere else to be laid down on our beds, we are very jealous of the fact that we are disease-free.

'Why have we suddenly got so much overfishing? Well, there are those who have moved into the area and think it's a quick way of making money. Then because of the appalling overfishing in the mackerel industry, those local fishermen who used to leave the oyster fishery and fish for mackerel re-rigged and came back for the oysters, hence another upsurge in the number of licences taken out.

'This might well be the day of the computer and scientist but they aren't the be-all and end-all of life and it didn't need scientific experts, just the evidence of your own eyes, to see what was happening. Nobody could bring those quantities of mackerel out of the sea and continue in that way. Those of us who said so have been proved right. You're up against big business of course but all you do is rape your own fishery.

1 'Crowst time' at East Pool tin mine (original photo by J. C. Burrow, 1893)

2 Old Levant tin mine (1880s). It was worked until 1919, when an accident to the beam engine resulted in a disaster which killed 31 men

3 *left* Changing shifts on the beam engine at Dolcoath mine (1893)

4 *above left and right* At the coal face

5 *below* Pit ponies

6 Pay day

7 A share-out

8 A miner's bath
9 The end of a miner's day

10 A Midland pit before the First World War

11 Velocipedes at Dinorwic Quarries, Llanberis (c. 1890)

12 Penrhyn Quarry, Bethesda:
working on the rock face
(c. 1913)

13 A Lowestoft fishing boat the
Chamois, running for
Newlyn in heavy weather
(1880s)

14 Herring girls at Lowestoft

15 Fish jousters packing and sorting fish at Newlyn (late 1870s)

16 *right*   Net mending at Vine Cottage, Boase Street in Newlyn
(original photo by Francis Frith)

17 Packing pilchards at Newlyn for export to Italy (1930s or late
1920s)

18 Mousehole harbour (1880s). Nets hung out after having been 'barked', i.e. dipped in a protective substance called *catechu*, known locally as 'cutch'

19 Making a coracle at Cenarth, Cardiganshire (c. 1930)

20 Coracle fishing at
Monmouth (c. 1890)

21 Shipbuilding at
Porthcressa in St
Mary's, Isles of Scilly
(1871): launch of the
David Auterson

22 Bunching flowers in
the early days on St
Mary's, Isles of Scilly

23 A threshing machine (1880s)

24 A two-horse hay sweep before the First World War

25 Haymaking in the early years of the twentieth century

26 George Lugg: hedger, ditcher and general labourer (1906)

27 Warwick 'Mop Fair' (one of the old hiring fairs)

28 Haymaking in Warwickshire (1880s)
29 Market day at Moreton in the Cotswolds (1880s)

30 Roasting a pig on a holiday in Moreton (1880s)

31 Herding sheep at Atherington, Devon (date unknown)

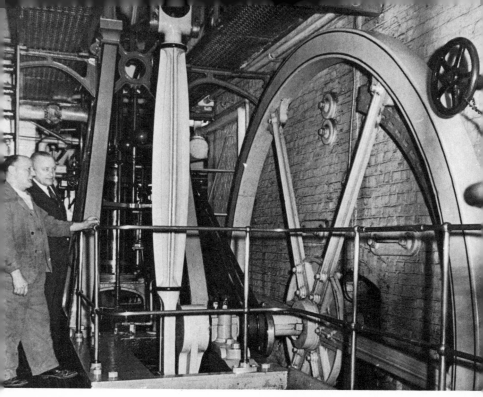

32 A Cornish beam engine at Young's Brewery
33 The farmyard at Young's Brewery

Well, it's happened here on a smaller scale but if the remedies the men themselves have promoted are put into operation then it might save the fishery. What is so commendable is that the people who actually earn a crust of bread there said they'd stop.

'There are three water bailiffs, including me, working on the fishery and checking the regulations are carried out, and the oysters are the right size. We get the odd cowboy, even the odd well-known one, that slips small oysters through, and there are those who say they are being taken from the fishery in massive quantities. I don't believe this. It is bound to happen to some extent, human nature being what it is and greed what it is and one man can't control eighty out there. But by and large I don't think it is the problem a lot of people make it out to be.

'Please God we have caught the problem of overfishing here in time. The men themselves have recognised it and they have one enormous advantage over the big fishermen outside — they are completely their own masters. They are independent fishermen and always want to be. When I first came I used to ask them why they didn't form co-operatives and make more money and they recognised they would, if they all got together, but it is such an individual enterprise, this fishing for oysters, that they are reluctant to let that go.

'When they go out in their smacks, no man's their master. They pay their licence fee, they obey the rules. No man is going to tell them what to do, how to fish. They are out there doing a traditional job in the way they like it because — let's face it — it's a lousy, filthy, back-breaking job. If you don't like it and know you aren't going to make a fortune, there must be other reasons why you do it.'

Henry Merrifield — a Lifetime on the Fal

The Fal winds its lazy way down from the city of Truro to the wide, natural harbour of Falmouth town. Along its banks are numerous creeks, some of which almost dry out at low water, and many villages with strange and attractive names — Playing Place, Come-to-Good and Devoran.

Henry Merrifield's foursquare granite house stands on the side of a steep hill above the river at Feock. The heart of his kitchen is the Rayburn on which the kettle constantly simmers and from his windows he can look out over the river beside which he has spent his 85 years, the river which has been his life. He is a widower.

'My wife died and my brother died four years ago on the same day and were buried the same day, the two of them. 'Course I'm not really old now. I'd an aunt who died just over the border [between Cornwall and Devon] and she was 105 and her sister, she was one of twins, I think she just made the 100. We're a long-lived family you see. Yet I can remember right back to when I was a little baby in the cradle.

'We had wooden rocking cradles then. I remember quite well being in the kitchen in the cradle and my mother walking about the house. I used to get hold of the cradle and rock it; apparently I was a big baby for my age even though I wasn't very old then. The other day I went to the shop for my paper and I'd just got to the top step when I heard a woman call, "you scamp!" I thought she spoke to me calling me a scamp, but it was to her dog and it reminded me of being a baby and my mother saying to me, when I rocked the cradle, "you scamp!" It don't seem long ago.

'I was born in the last cottage right down by the river. My father was a fisherman but in the summertime he would go away to sea. He was a big man and he had his ticket, a second mate's ticket, but he wanted to study for to be first mate and he used to study wintertime when he was home. He'd have all his books laid out on the table when we had a fire in the front room (as we used to call it) and we all had to keep very quiet when those books came out.

'My father died when I was only 11. He was on a boat abroad somewhere and went swimming and got some kind of a fever which affected his heart. He came home but he died when he was only 46. It was hard on my mother, left with four children, my brother who was older then me and I'd a sister each side of me. My uncle first took me on the Fal.'

Henry has his uncle's oyster fishing licence for 1869, price 3s.

'I suppose it was about then I started oystering, in the September I was 11. I went out with my brother in a small boat. My father had had a bigger boat, 28 feet long, but after he died it was laid up. The small boat was all right in fine weather but it was very hard work when it was rough particularly at the age we were. My father had looked to the future when he'd had the big boat built, when the three of us could fish; it was very sad as he died after he'd only had her for two seasons.

'I've never worked for anyone ashore in my life. I started then and I was always on the water. We'd good seasons and bad seasons when I first went oystering but things were so different then. When I first fished as a boy, oysters was about half a crown to 5s. a thousand, a *thousand*. But, of course, money was different too from what it is now. You could get a dozen boxes of matches for a penny, cigarettes were five a penny and tobacco was about 3d. an ounce (that's the old pence) and coal about 9d. a hundredweight. When you look at it the wages people are getting now, and the price of things, then they're no better off than they were in the old days. A pound was worth a pound then.

'The big job in those early days was getting the oysters away to sell them but we was fortunate as my brother had a man to take his oysters. He used to sell them up in Plymouth to the French, but then a lot of the merchants were French in those days, and Dutch. At the end of the season we'd take up the final load ourselves by boat to Falmouth docks and send them off by train.

'Our first little boat was a rowing boat and that was really hard work. You see when you dredge oysters under sail, the movement of the boat do do the dredging but in a small boat you just have to heave and put your dredge over, then pull her along and handwinch it up. Once we'd decided we were big enough to take out the sailing boat we wished we'd done it much earlier.

'I remember when one family − I won't tell you who − tried to dredge in a boat with a motor. They went out for three or four hours and by the end of the day, by jingo, they'd a big quantity of oysters compared to what we would get and then the next day, even though the weather was bad, they went out again and they said we couldn't stop that boat because they'd got a licence.

'You can imagine the dissatisfaction among the other fishermen, and they made it a rule then that no one could fish under mechanical power. If they hadn't there wouldn't be no oysters left at all now. I remember my uncle telling me how Truro City came to look after the fishery. Many years back, my uncle and those older than him told me that when they came in first there was no such regulations and the fisherman on the fishery would appoint so many to look after it. But then it got that nobody was volunteering to do it so they thought it was better to go to a corporate body than to an individual or half a dozen or so, so they put it to the Corporation in Truro and they agreed to look after it.

'When I first started on the fishing, of course, the tin mines were still working and they were all going at the top there, around Hal Dhu. All the waste used to come down through Devoran River to Restronguet and into the Fal. It would make the oysters go green and when they had them analysed they found copper, zinc and tin in them so when we used to sell them they'd be taken up to Plymouth and put in pure water tanks in the river Yealm while they cleared though the French would buy them anyway.

'But I reckon they were harmless and I'll tell you why. We used to do what we called overwinter then. That is, keep oysters back from one season to sell them at the beginning of the next when they were a better price. My uncle used to keep such oysters in one part of the creek, in shallow water which would dry out in the daytimes so that he could get to them at suitable times. Every night when the tide was right he'd go off down there to look at his oysters by the light of his hurricane lamp. I used to go down there with him.

'Now my uncle kept a cat and that cat would go with him every time he visited his oysters and he used to give her an oyster. She was mad for oysters. So I reckon if those oysters had been poisoned then it would have killed that cat as she must have eaten hundreds going down there nearly every day for years on end.

'You were considered fortunate if you could afford to overwinter oysters. I remember my brother and I asking some fellow why he didn't put some away for the next season and he looked at us as if we were mad. He'd a wife and family, you see, and he couldn't afford to. We were thoughtless as we were just two young bachelor fellows then.

'In those days the ring was smaller than it is now. It was 2¼". I was strictly not allowed to catch them smaller but even in those days some tried and I remember two chaps being sent up the line [i.e. to prison] for it. When my uncle was a boy a man could be fined £20 or more for doing it and that really was a lot of money then. It was a terrible scandal too as it all went in the newspaper.

'We used to call a good fishing place a "bal".'

Henry did not know why and it is strange as the word bal means a mine.

'You'd go back and say there's a real bal out there today. You'd go off out with the dredges. They are made of an iron triangle with a knife at the bottom and they taper away to a ring. The knife is dragged along the bottom and dredges along the ground over the floor − the shells of whelks and dead oysters and so on. The bottom of the net would be wire and the top twine before the nylon and terylene nets. We made them ourselves and they would get very torn. It was unusual if a net lasted a season. Then you pulled out the dredge and had to "cull" the oysters, that is sort them out from the shells. You had to be very careful as sometimes they would catch under the ring when you put them through it and you had to be careful not to damage the shell by handling them. They've only got a shell like a fingernail, very thin, and if they get too damaged they'll die. Also if they were chipped then the buyers wouldn't like them though they'd know if they were caught legally or not. They say centuries back you could catch them at an inch and a half. My uncle had half a dozen different-sized rings.

'I kept on fishing until I was nearly 80. I'd good health, you see. Then last winter I got rheumatism. The worst of it is I get cold feet now. I got two pairs of stockings and I do wear paper socks to keep warm and my daughter told me to always keep the fire going. I get rheumatism in the shoulder especially when there's rain. I always know when there will be rain − it never fails.

'It's a bad thing, now, the fishing. There's too many of them at it, and they've grown too greedy. I've seen them putting oysters away for sale recently less than 2" across; if you go on like that there'll be no fishery left.

'You see oysters is a mystery. Sometimes I heard my uncle say he'd drifted from one end of the fishery to the other for one or two oysters. Then he'd go out and catch perhaps a thousand or two in a day, sometimes even more. It all depends where you go and how you take them. But oysters is a mystery I don't think anybody can understand.'

Jack Harvey

The one sea creature which still appears to be plentiful is the crab and the Harvey brothers of Newlyn have been selling shellfish all their working lives. Their family has been doing it for as long as they can remember. In 1955 the family set up a little wholesaling business, using one old stone fish loft on the Coombe, and it began to make them a nice little living. Then, in the last three or four years, business just boomed.

'On a single day now,' says Jack Harvey, 'our boys will be boiling 10,000 lbs of crabs in the boilers.' There are seven lofts, twenty-five girls are employed to clean the shellfish and they have just completed tanks on the quay to contain live shellfish awaiting shipment. 'We now have the finest storage system for live shellfish in the British Isles.'

The cause of the boom is a huge export trade.

'We began by exporting crayfish, never a favourite in this country. Almost all of them go to France and the lorry loads set off weekly to cross on the Plymouth-Roscoff ferry.

'You know, the crayfish is one of the true mysteries of the sea. You hardly ever catch one less than 3 pounds in weight, whether you net them, pot them, dive for them, anything. That means they are at least 7 years old, most are 15 to 20 years old. They have ringed them to try and find out their habits and they only move a mile or so in years. So what happens to the young crayfish? Nobody knows. Ninety eight per cent of crayfish are caught off the Cornish coast, possibly because of the warm waters of the Gulf Stream.

'Fishermen used to say the crayfish have "come in" but that doesn't seem to be the case as it appears they are there all the time. But their life cycle is a mystery and they are getting very rare so the price is good.'

We talked among mountains of crabs, with lobsters scuttling around the floor and the telephone ringing continually. At five-minute intervals fishermen arrived with shellfish. 'We have five boats of our own but at least another hundred fish full-time for us. See that smartly dressed young man over there? Never seen him before in my life.' He paid him in cash.

'People bring us fish all the time. We pay the top going rate, no more and no less. I pay for every catch on the spot in cash.

'Crayfish are now fished for by boats using tiers of nets, perhaps ten to thirty tiers each about 600 yards long. This is fine for crayfish but lobsters and crabs can get mangled so it is still a question of using pots and bait to get them in the best condition.'

Lobsters go mainly to the London restaurants. There have been plenty of them in recent years and Harveys were paying the fishermen (in 1982) £2 per pound live weight. Harveys own mark-up varies from 10 to 15 per cent 'which is fine for us'. He muses, though, on the profits along the line and just who does make them when a lobster thermidor in a restaurant will set you back £8.50p even in the west country and that is only for half a lobster.

'But our major export now is crabs, it's really expanded. Some 7,800 kilos a week are currently leaving us for Scandinavia alone where they are very fond of them but where they are scarce because the water is too cold. We have devised an elaborate preserving system for the crabs which are not frozen but pasteurised and kept at a temperature just a degree above freezing. They will keep for four weeks like this.'

Holland, too, buys crabs and huge Dutch and French lorries arrive in Newlyn. They have massive water tanks full of seawater which is constantly aerated by a pump worked from the engine. 'The French particularly like spider crabs which are often used only as bait by fishermen here. Scandinavians go for the common female crab, especially when it is full of roe; that is the dark meat many British restaurants dislike.'

Above him, in a long room, girls disentangle crab meat from mounds and mounds of crabs. It is all done by hand, a fiddly and messy job. The crab meat is then made into blocks and frozen for use in the winter or when the weather is too bad for the boats to go out.

Yet greed is here too, somewhere along the line. Crab is no longer cheap even in a place where cheap crab sandwiches used to be a feature of local life. Harveys still sell crabs relatively cheaply directly to buyers from their fish loft so a hefty profit must be made somewhere along the line. I asked about the possibility of overfishing.

Said Jack Harvey,

'At the moment they are so plentiful it is like picking blackberries on the moor. There are three of us brothers working here now, along with our four sons. We work from the small hours of the morning until we see the fish lorries away late at night.

'The new tanks on the quay mean that the fish can be sorted into sizes, sexes and grades and prospective buyers can see what is there at a glance. Fish that look as if they are not going to last can be hooked out.'

Alone among the fishermen and fishing businesses of Newlyn, the Harveys are optimistic about the future so long as the supply of crabs remains plentiful. Nobody dare mention what might happen if it does not.

11

Colliers, cockles and coracles

There are many similarities between Cornwall and West Wales, from the language to the type of coastline. The two areas are also beset with the same problems, high unemployment and a drift by the young up the country as the chance of jobs recede and the small cottages are bought up by second-home owners and for the holiday trade – a practice which has brought about violent action in Wales.

Fishing was never the stable industry in West Wales that it was in West Cornwall but certain areas produced their own delicacies and the Welsh cockle provided a living for one small town. Ironically, while both Cornwall and West Wales have set out to attract the holidaymaker as a means of bringing in income and employment, the very ease of travel brought about by the car has its own problems – some small Welsh holiday resorts have now almost become forgotten as today's tourists race by along the main roads.

And years ago the coalminers were only too glad to get two weeks' holiday in a village on the west coast, whereas now they are more likely to take package trips to Majorca and the Costa Brava.

Also clinging on for survival in West Wales are those fishermen who still use one of the oldest fishing methods known throughout the world – these are the coracle fishermen of the Towy and Taf rivers, still using their round boats although they can no longer make a full-time living out of it.

The House of Commons

Llanstephan is a tiny village on the estuary of the River Towy, not far from Carmarthen. It is a very quiet place, attracting only a handful of summer visitors and a few touring holidaymakers who stop off to climb up to the castle before continuing on their way to Laugharne or Pembroke.

At the turn of the century, it was bustling. It had two industries, holidaymaking and cockles, and both have virtually gone. From the flat sandy beach you can look across to Ferryside where a small railway still runs and from where the holidaymakers used to visit Llanstephan by boat.

Ocky Owen, the tiny village barber, retired from barbering at the age of 80. For years his small wooden hut, in the very centre of the village, was the centre of village life and it was known as the House of Commons.

Now he lives by himself in a fine Victorian house which has become too big for him and remembers the busy days before the First World War.

'My father came from Whitland and my dear mother from Login. They used to make a joke about Login. Two men were going along in a train wondering where they were going to stay, when they went through a station. "Look," said one to the other, "we'll be all right if we get out here — it says lodgin'." I was born here, right in Llanstephan, the eighth of nine children. That's why I was called Octavius. It was no joke having nine children in those days but we were all very well looked after and had a good start in life.

'Anyway my father had not intended to take up barbering but he did it because there was no one else doing it. I didn't choose it either. My brother went up to London and made a name for himself in the big hotels and so I went up there before the First War to work and train with him. There wasn't much choice then, I mean you couldn't just decide to go into a profession or decide what kind of a job you might like, not unless you were well off.

'In those days, before the war, this place was packed with visitors. The influx of visitors was so tremendous it was like a miniature Piccadilly here. There'd be crowds and crowds out walking the streets at twelve o'clock at night. I don't know whether it's just fancy but it seems the weather was better then than it is today. They do say it goes in cycles and if so then those summers before 1914 were one of the good cycles.

'You can't imagine what the sheer numbers were like then. You'd sell six to eight dozen walking sticks in one day. We used to get postcards in, printed in Germany and coloured. They cost 1d. with a halfpenny stamp. People would buy perhaps four to six *dozen* postcards while they were here and write to everybody. You see it's the car that finished the village as a holiday resort. In the old days everyone would come down by train to Ferryside and then they would come over on the ferry and they would be here for a fortnight, so they would have plenty of time to write. Not like today when they come through in a car for half an hour and buy one card.

'Then we might sell two dozen pairs of bathing trunks each day, cigarettes not by the thousand – by the ton. A haircut cost 3d. and a shave 2d. I remember some cross old man coming back here one very hot day and he was sweating. He said to my father, "why didn't you remind me I hadn't paid you – two pence for a shave." My father said it didn't matter, he could have paid again but the man was still cross. "2d. is 2d.," he said, "and I've had to walk back all this way to pay it." They were like that then.

'The pubs would be open at six in the morning and by seven they would be full with the colliers. Many of the holiday-makers were colliers and their families from the Rhondda. Do you know what they would drink? Rum and warm milk. It was to strengthen them you see for the next twelve months' work underground. I remember one little man putting on thirteen pounds in fourteen days, just like an old horse put out to grass. Rum and milk was sold by the gallon – I've seen many a supposed teetotaller drunk by nine o'clock in the morning.

'We could have two fairs come at the weekends and there would be stalls at the roadside selling books and papers, buckets and spades, drinks, everything revolved around the **village**.

'Then for a hundred years we'd the mock mayor making — what a great day that was! It would be advertised for days beforehand and the crowds would come in, not by lorries or buses or anything then, of course, but on foot or by horse and trap. There'd be such a huge crowd out in the woods they'd shout at them through loudspeakers. The mock mayor was made for a year and it was always a visitor who was elected.

'This was a show for the visitors, it was *their* day. One of the popular visitors was chosen, often because of his good singing. They used to have singing going on all the time then in the woods. I remember one very popular mayor, a Dr Jones from Merthyr Tydfil, a proper professional doctor. Then he'd march through the town with all the crowds and the town band, and people with their ponies, and scores of children. The children would be blowing away on kazoos.

'The children's band was led by old Shilty, a man who was very fond of the drink. I can see him now as he was one year, an old silk top hat on his head which must not have been hired out previous to that for fifty years, and he stopped all the kids and said, in Welsh and excuse my language in translation, "now my dear children, here's the mayor, blow up the bloody band, blow it to hell with it. . . ." '

The war came and Ocky, back from London, volunteered. 'I was graded C3 for home duties only. But as time went on, everyone had to go and I was called up. When I got to France the doctor said I should never have been sent but by then it was too late, we were there.

'It was indescribable. I hardly ever talk about it. War cannot be described, it's got to be lived and experienced. We had only five weeks' training then we were sent from regiment to regiment, eight regiments in fourteen days, as replacements, ending with the Northumberland Fusiliers at Passchaendale. Passchaendale — hell's own fairyland, the place where the sun never shone, where men were eaten with lice and clothed in mud, and lay down to take their rest in shell holes. Some of the people I knew then haunt me still. I still weep when I think of them.'

On 18 October 1917 Ocky was wounded, 'and I remember walking straight through the firing for perhaps 200 or 300 yards as the dawn was breaking and nothing else hitting me.' He was in hospital six months and invalided home, still ill and 'with my nerves completely shattered. It was all so senseless, it was to no purpose at all, but then war is never to any purpose.'

He set up again as a barber

'though I was so nervous at first that I used to sweat with fear. But it got better and then I met my dear wife, Esther. She was teaching in the village and she had two sisters, three such lovely girls you never saw. In the end we all lived together as such a happy family. My brother told my parents who had then been married sixty-seven years that they would never want for anything. "They were looked after like the King and Queen of England." But that's how the old people were treated then, not pushed away into homes.'

For nearly sixty years Ocky ran the House of Commons.

'People used to come and confide all their problems, all their troubles. Sometimes they just wanted to talk, sometimes they'd ask advice and they knew I'd never say anything. I knew the secrets of the hearts of many men. I had some simple rules; no swearing — except for damn, that was fair enough; no quarrels, if there was any quarrelling it had to be settled outside, then they must come back in and shake hands and not refer to it again; no rows over politics.

'Men would come back with their sons, grandsons and great-grandsons. I used to keep a little stick for cheeky children and if they were really naughty I'd give them a hit on the bottom and their mothers would usually send them back afterwards to apologise.'

As the holiday trade began to die away it still left Llanstephan and the tiny hamlet outside, Llangain, with the cockles. Carmarthenshire cockles were a great delicacy, sought after all over West Wales and taken to Swansea and Cardiff to be sold in the markets and from door to door.

'Two or three families lived just by cockles in Llanstephan, and most of the people of Llangain. They would come down with their ponies and donkeys and work the beaches. It would all be done by hand with a little scraper and it was hard work and often cold and wet but it made them a decent living, not a rich living, but a decent living. There was enough cockles for everybody, they never ran short.

'It went on like that until ten or so years ago then this man came from Laugharne who reckoned he'd the rights to the beach. He came down on the beach with bulldozers. They told me there were cockles there by the millions then and that he was paying people £100 a week to pick them up after the bulldozer had scraped the beach. He was a very, very greedy man.

'Then, one night, the storm came – and in a single night the cockles all went. And they have never come back.

'So they made a rich living for a little time, cockles by the hundreds of sackfuls and now those poor people who made a steady small living out of them have been denied it. It's all greed. Self first, self last and if there's anything over then it's self again.

'It's hard to describe the changes now, it is so great. We were truly religious then. I remember my dear wife as a young girl, going with her sister to Llanelli. When they set out on the ferry the sun was shining like diamonds on the clear water but when she got back the water was grey and rough and when they reached the ferry boat they could hear quarrelling. The ferryman was waving his oar at some of the passengers who wanted to get out of the boat. Anyway they got in, in fear and trembling, and they set out, and my wife asked her sister what they could do, get out? Her sister said they couldn't so they'd better pray. So they did and the only prayer they could think of was "Be present at our table, Lord". Anyway the Lord didn't mind and they got back safe and sound.

'Not long ago someone said to me how hard it was "in the olden days" and I said I wasn't sure at all. There was a certain contentment then, in some ways life was easier even if the work was harder. 10s. was worth 10s. This place was thriving with the visitors coming for three months. People could accumulate a bit of money for the winter when times were hard and life was a struggle; and then we'd the cockles too.

'Nowadays you see disasters every time you put on the television. In those days you were let down more gently, you'd to walk three miles to buy a newspaper. They say we are civilised yet we are nearer catastrophe than ever. We're obsessed now with making money, just to pile it in the banks for the mildew and the cobwebs to get it — what good is it beyond what anybody needs to meet their wants? You read in the papers of someone dying intestate leaving £30,000, £75,000, what the devil for? Presumably for the Devil.

'I think of that happy, busy household with my old parents, my wife and I, her two sisters, children, friends. Now there's just myself and one sister left out of the nine children of our family and my wife and her two sisters are both dead. I've never had to live on my own before. You come into an empty house and wait for a voice to call your name and it doesn't come. They say you have your memories but that makes it sadder. In those supposed hard old times you lived with your family when you were old and you were part of a busy village full of life. It's all gone and they call it progress.'

Fishing in Merlin's river

Carmarthen town is a curious mixture of old streets, local authority offices and new building. It has its market and pubs but into the streets are creeping the chain stores and anonymous shop fronts which make all town centres look alike these days.

Yet its history is an old one. Carmarthen is allegedly Merlin's town and legend has it that he lies buried in a cave under a hill, Bryn Myrddin, above it. In fact, until 1979, Merlin's oak — just a stump — stood on a street corner and that too had a legend.

> When this oak shall tumble down,
> Then will fall Carmarthen town.

Merlin is severally said to have been the son of a Celtic prince, the son of a prince of darkness or a local river god and certainly the river and water have played a part in his legend. It is said that should he be disturbed the town would be destroyed by floods. In fact, when the council did remove the stump (said by some anyway to be merely the remains of a tree planted on the site in 1704 and poisoned by a previous worthy to deter souvenir hunters), Merlin or someone sent a flash flood down the river Towy which flooded half the town.

If Merlin did exist with a real life King Arthur, somewhere around the fourth or fifth centuries A.D., then coracle fishing would have been well established in his day. In fact, so far as it is possible to know the little skin boats with their unique steering method were out and about on British rivers long before the Roman conquest.

Coracle fishing is, arguably, the oldest form of trawl fishing in the world. The beam trawl — where the net is held open by a beam making a kind of pocket into which the fish will swim — has been in use for centuries but trawling from a coracle goes back way beyond that. The little round skin boat is one of the most primitive crafts man has ever devised and it is worked in pairs. The men paddle up the river and then float down, running a net between them. The impetus of the movement keeps the mouth of the trawl net open and the fish, hopefully, swim in to it.

Coracle fishers are now few in number and may not survive much longer. The first threat to the Carmarthen fishers was the building of the enormous Llyn Brianne reservoir which taps the head waters of the River Towy. It is one of the largest reservoirs in Europe and in spite of all the promises made at the time, it has had a drastic effect on the Towy waters and this, in turn, has had a direct effect on the fish.

An informant had told me I could not miss the coracle men, their appearance was so remarkable. 'I was driving along the river bank in the gloom,' he had said, 'and suddenly I saw these creatures straight out of a science fiction nightmare — kind of tortoise men. . . .' What he had seen had been the coracle fishers on their way down to the river carrying their boats in the traditional way, on their backs and supported by a leather strap across their chests.

Raymond Rees cannot quite trace his ancestry back to the time of Merlin but it certainly goes back beyond the time when records were kept in the town at all. The coracle fishing skill has been passed along the line from father to son so long as anyone can remember. Now he is pessimistic.

'The flow from the reservoir has reduced the flow up the banks and made the water dirty. Salmon and sewin (sea trout), the mainstay of us coracle men, dislike dirty water and so they avoid it. They also like strong-flowing water of a fair depth and sometimes now the Towy is reduced to just a trickle of its former self.'

The row, he says, has boiled on for a long time between fishermen, amateur and professional, and the various water authorities who claim that their sensitive instruments registered sufficient water in the river for the fish. It is a familiar story — heard by the Newlyn fishermen from the lips of Government experts in Whitehall who told them the mackerel was not being overfished.

'Now it seems we have won our case too late,' says Raymond Rees.

'During the first two weeks of August last year [1980] two "floods" of 300 million gallons were allowed into the Towy and from now on 150 million additional gallons will come down every other weekend. Sensitive instruments is it? What good are they when you could see what was happening to the river with your own eyes.

'The second hazard is the drilling for the pillars of the new bridge for yet another by-pass for Carmarthen, slap in the middle of our coracle run. The contractors were told by the river authority that there was no objection. It's unbelievable. We objected back in 1969 when the idea was first mooted. It's ludicrous in this day and age that a single span bridge can't be built. The widest point of the river here — and that's across from bank top to bank top — is only forty feet. There will then be five bridges crossing the Towy in half a mile. Each one collects more mud and silt and makes it that much more difficult but the new one comes right in the best and deepest part of the run.'

There are still twelve pairs of coracles operating on the Towy at Carmarthen, a couple more further down at St Cleers and a small number on the river Teify in Cardiganshire, although there most of the true rights were sold during the Depression in the 1930s. Fishermen, frantic to get enough money on which to live, sold out to businessmen and fishing clubs and now you can buy a permit to fish the Teify.

'In Carmarthen the rights still pass on down the family from father to son, right down the centuries and when a family dies out the permits die out with them. We do not sell them,' says Raymond.

You can see him and his partner bobbing down the river in his minute boat on a dark night of heavy rain. It looks very precarious. The coracle run passes down the river where the banks have become blighted and dismal; old ruined warehouses jostle with heaps of rubble, a new road brings heavy trunk traffic roaring by while sodium lights throw a lurid glow over the whole scene.

Down in the water are the little pairs of boats, so unchanged since the Romans came to colonise Merlin's town, the fine net runs out skilfully between them, the two men working together as one without a word being spoken between them. The nets are 33 feet long and about 2 foot 6 inches deep and the men still make them themselves. They used to be made of horsehair but now it is nylon.

Boat materials too have changed as Raymond says,

'There are still some of the really old boats being used, made of calico painted with pitch and tar and stretched over willow frames. It was easy, see, until a few years ago. There was a gasworks here then — now it's finished and it's all North Sea Gas — and you could get your pitch from them. Then there was a sawmill — now ruined — with a travelling bench and you could take in your own tree and have it cut up into strips. But that's all gone. So modern boats have to be made of fibre glass to the old patterns.'

He explained how the fishing works.

'At dusk the fishers draw lots to determine who goes first.

The first man pairs with the next, the next two follow on and so on. But that's quite new. Before they pulled down the houses along this part of the river and stuck a by-pass there, we used the system they had used for many centuries. The first man to get here put his coracle and net on the river, marking where he wanted it to start, and nobody touched it. He waited until he could count seven stars in the sky and then he could begin, once the next man had arrived. The third would pair with the fourth and so on. Once they opened up this river bank though, vandals would come down and jump on the coracles until they were smashed or steal the stick (a kind of club used to knock the fish on the head) and so it all had to stop; dreadful, isn't it, after all that time?

'Until this terrible mania for redevelopment hit Carmarthen, the river was a thriving area of houses, pubs, river walks and sawmills, nothing like the derelict wasteland it has become today. The council moved the families out and promised them modern new houses with a nice view of the river. But what did they build in the only place possible? A bloody great police station. . . . They destroyed the whole heart of the town. The river *was* Carmarthen. Instead of building on the town's natural advantages, we've got a monstrous great shopping precinct half empty and the loss of the old market building. The story of our town's redevelopment has become famous.

'Coracle fishermen can no longer make a full-time living from the fishing any more. Most of us have to have other jobs. I have a fish stall in what remains of the market. I'm the secretary of the Coracle Fishers' Association and this post has come down to me in a direct line from my grandfather and his grandfather before him. Permits go back to the mid-1800s but the same names were to be found fishing on this river in coracles long before that time. We know all about hard times in Carmarthen but we didn't give in like some of the others and sell out to the highest bidder.

'In fact I heard that some chap in the town who claims to belong to a family whose permit has lapsed wrote to Prince Charles as Prince of Wales and asked him to ask his dad to ask me to give him a licence! He said he thought the prince would be interested in the survival of coracle fishing as he was a "patron of the arts". Coracle fishing being, he said, an art form. . . . He can ask who he likes, all he likes for as long as he likes but there's not trace of his name on my lists for the last 150 years or so. The Prince of Wales is welcome to come along and see for himself.'

12

The islanders

The problems besetting the Scilly Isles are those which have faced all our island communities. They also, in some part, provide a microcosm of what has happened to the mainland communities once dependent on one, or at the most two, small industries.

The number of people living on our offshore islands has dwindled — apart from the oil-rich Shetlands. Whole communities have been forcibly removed in the past, notably from St Kilda off the west coast of Scotland and Samson in the Scillies. Life on an exposed island has, until recent years, been a very hard one. Now their economies are being stifled by the high cost of transport and fuel when nearly every necessity has to be freighted in.

The Scillies lie nearly 30 miles off Land's End, in the western approaches. They are blessed with an exceptionally mild climate as the Gulf Stream washes around their shores. There are now five inhabited islands, the largest and most populous being St Mary's; the others are St Agnes, St Martin's, Tresco and Bryher. At one time St Mary's, St Martin's, Tresco and Bryher were joined together, as were some of the smaller islands such as the Eastern Isles. Geologists and archaeologists agree that they had separated, as the land sunk, by around 600 B.C. Those four islands form a ring around a shallow lagoon, while St Agnes has always been separated by a channel of deep water.

As well as the inhabited islands, which used to include the island of Samson, there are literally dozens of smaller ones varying from large rocks to islands such as Nor-Nour where you can see the remains of iron-age houses some of which are below today's tideline. The high points on the west of the islands are rich in passage graves — archaeologists do not know whether native Scillonians only were buried here or whether great chiefs were brought over from the mainland to be buried in graves facing across the magnificent sky and seascape of the Atlantic.

Because of their position, the islands were notorious for wrecks. Some of these are well known, such as the wreck of the *Association*, Sir Cloudesley Shovel's flagship, in 1707, along with the *Eagle* and the *Romney*, but there were very many more. Today's Scillonians stoutly deny ever having gone in for deliberate wrecking but wrecks did provide material help for those living a hard life. There is an old prayer which says that while 'we do not pray for wrecks we pray that if there be any, then they be guided into the Isles of Scilly for the benefit of the poor inhabitants.'

One of the earliest stories told about the wreck of the *Association* is how Sir Cloudesley's body was washed ashore at Porthellick Cove on St Mary's. It had been assumed he was dead when he reached the shore but it is said that many years later, a dying island woman confessed to her priest that she had found the admiral alive but faint and had murdered him for his valuables, including a fine emerald ring she had pulled off his finger with her teeth.

Whatever the truth of that story the islanders bravely rescued hundreds of people over the years from certain death. They provided pilots for centuries, rowing out to ships in their famous pilot gigs. Politically they have remained loyal to the crown. Henry VIII built a fort on St Mary's to fight off pirates; in 1571 Queen Elizabeth sent over Francis Godolphin as Governor and the fine Star Castle was built as a defence against the Spanish. The Scillies hung on for the monarchy after the Civil War ended and Cromwell was also forced to send over troops — his own small castle, Cromwell's Castle, can still be seen on Tresco.

The islanders scraped a living from the land, from kelp, the seaweed burned in kilns to make a soda ash which was exported to the soap and glass factories on the mainland. Other industries rose and fell, pilotage being one. Boatbuilding kept the inhabitants of St Mary's in work until the coming of steam — it was too expensive to build ships with boilers and engines. But as each industry passed away, the islanders were left in dire straits, especially those on the off islands.

Then came the first major change. In 1843 Augustus Smith, a Hereford gentleman, was granted a lease on the islands. He called himself Lord Proprietor of the Isles and he was to rule there as an uncrowned king for thirty-seven years. Opinions are still extremely divided about him. He was certainly an autocrat. But he did realise the potential of the islands' climate, laid the foundations of the early flower and vegetable industries and introduced compulsory education into Scilly long before it existed on the mainland by the simple expedient of charging each family one penny per child per week to go to school and two pennies if they did not go.

The Dorrien-Smith family still hold Tresco which has become a holiday island for the wealthy. The Duchy of Cornwall owns the rest, apart from the town of Hugh Town. Over the last century tourism has gradually taken over from everything else, change accelerating rapidly during the last ten years but, as we shall see from the accounts that follow, not only has it proved a very mixed blessing but it also appears, for a whole variety of reasons, that it could face the same kind of rapid demise that has occurred with all the successive industries on which the islanders have depended for their livelihoods.

When I first visited Scilly, as a child, in 1947, vehicles were almost unknown. By some roadsides you would see what appeared to be an old, rusty wreck of an engine, roped on to a rusty chassis on wheels with tyres from which most of the rubber had long since gone. It was an amazing sight, therefore, when the ferry docked to see these vehicles actually being driven down to the quay. Now there are large expensive cars although there seems little point — only St Mary's has a made up road and the entire circuit of it is only nine miles.

There has also been a rash of new building, strictly limited however for lack of space. The Duchy of Cornwall allowed its tenants, in Hugh Town on St Mary's, to buy their houses as sitting tenants and that, say today's Scillonians, was the beginning of the rot. Too many got greedy and sold out at high prices, bringing about the spiralling costs which puts a small cottage beyond the reach of any islander — £70,000 is an average 1982 price for a two-bedroomed cottage.

While most of the accounts in this book are drawn from memories of the very old, this is not so in this chapter. Many of the old Scillonians have left the islands for the mainland — priced out. The young go too in search of work. I wish I had taken note of some of the old stories years ago for on one of my early trips I met an old lady, long since dead, whose grandmother had been the last baby born on the now uninhabited island of Samson. So much has the pattern of life become disrupted as islanders have moved away and entrepreneurs from the mainland moved in, along with the wealthy buying cottages as second homes, that there is nobody left who can even remember surely the history of Samson.

The accounts that follow come from Alf Jenkins, master mariner, whose family have been seafarers out of Scilly since anyone can remember. He has become a local historian in his own right. The Gibson family have become famous for their remarkable collection of wreck photographs, dating back from the earliest days of photography (although most date back no earlier than the 1860s). Other comments come from local people and from the schoolteachers who have to prepare the islands' children for a life on the mainland. The continuity of life and of oral history has become disjointed, and I have given a very brief account of the islands' past to give some understanding of the stories to come.

Alf Jenkins lives in a small terraced cottage in the middle of Hugh Town. Its front faces the tiny, triangular patch of ground known as the park. Its back is towards the harbour. Successions of summer visitors stop and take photographs of his magnificent sub-tropical front garden, crammed to over-flowing with the plants which do so well in Scilly such as mesembryanthemums and Livingstone daisies. They carpet the walls and flower beds in scarlet, orange, rose pink and bright yellow, while behind them huge succulents and ice plants rise in banks to the pink and scarlet climbing geraniums which smother the house walls.

'You almost came too late to hear about the history of Scilly. I reckon that in twenty years there won't be a Scillonian left on the islands. Only forty native families remain — and that includes all the off islands as well as St Mary's. People from the mainland have bought in to the town just to make money or for holiday homes — in this one tiny place ninety-eight houses stand empty for three-quarters of the year. In the winter it's terrible, it's just like a ghost town, there's no life left at all.

'Even four or five years ago there were plenty of old people who could tell you stories about life in the islands, now there's precious few. When I was writing my book on the pilot cutters and gigs I would go and chat to the old men and they would try and remember their names. If you asked them outright how many they could remember they couldn't tell you but when they chatted together one would say something like, "do you remember the old yellow one, the Misletoe?" and another would say, "that weren't the Misletoe, she was painted green, perhaps you're thinking of the Dolly Varden", and that's how I found out about many of them.

'Some things have gone completely in my lifetime. No one any longer seems to know the history of Samson for example.' I was told, years ago, that the island became uninhabited some time in the nineteenth century after all the menfolk were drowned on a rescue mission to a boat off the Wolf Rock. The women could no longer manage on this small, barren island and left. It appears there is some doubt as to what happened when.

'The Samson people were the beatniks of Scilly, or I suppose you might say the outlaws. After the Civil War, when the Godolphins came back as Governors, they brought the Mumford family with them (they've been here ever since). The Mumfords were pretty officious by all accounts in those days and they rode around on big horses telling people what to do. Well some of the St Mary's families, like the Webbers and the Woodcocks, removed themselves over to Samson and lived there.

'There were never many on the island. An old rent book shows twelve households in 1715. Nobody knows when the disaster happened but an old schoolteacher here, a Miss Tiddy, she said that she had always been told it was in 1801 and that the Samson men had boarded a French privateer. They were told to sail it to Plymouth and it was on the way to Plymouth that all the Samson men, nineteen adults and boys, were drowned when the ship hit the Wolf Rock in a gale.

'However it couldn't have been then that the island became uninhabited because there are rent books after that and twice, in 1836 and 1842, they bought pilot cutters. Both were later wrecked and in 1856 Mr Augustus Smith ordered the families off. They had to take them off by force — that's something that is remembered.

'There's a strange story about it too. The legend goes that old Mrs Woodcock wouldn't leave at first. She told Mr Smith to push off. They say she was something of a witch. Anyway Mr Smith told her she'd be taken away by force if she didn't go of her own accord and two men went to take her away to the boat. They say that she fixed them, and Mr Smith, with her eye and they stood there transfixed, paralysed, until she had got aboard the boat in her own good time. . . .'

At low tide you can see stone walls running between Samson and the other islands. Archaeologists say they are the remains of fields from the Iron Age, before the land sank. Mr Jenkins says they were fish traps. Probably both are correct, the Samson islanders using old walls that had been there for centuries.

'My great grandfather, Long John Jenkins, says he was told by one of the old Webbers that the first job the children had to do of a morning on Samson was to empty out the traps. The walls could be filled in with clay to make them waterproof, the tide would come in over the top with fish, and then fall away and you'd be left with the fish.'

Alf makes no bones about the fact that for centuries the Scillonians supplemented their income with smuggling.

'Just about every family on all the islands was involved, men and women. Even the parson got caught for it — it's there in the records for September 1826, King against the Chaplain and seven others, with a fine of £90. 14s. It was said that in the heyday of smuggling more contraband was landed in Scilly than at the Customs and Excise warehouse in London.'

Among the records Alf has is a set of documents from Penzance on the mainland. One letter from an excise officer to London explains how he had set about stamping out smuggling in the islands and that, 'I had hoped its total extinction was not far distant, more especially as the old smuggling establishments were broken up and none but the lowest of the people engaged in it.' However, in a further report, having told of the smugglers having pulled off a huge haul of spirits (600 gallons) and tobacco (3000 lbs), he says, 'after this successful landing in the face of the most efficient guard that ever has been, or I believe one can devise, I despair of any means being found to put a stop to it even when accompanied by the most severe penalties. . . .'

For many years pilotage, says Alf, was the major occupation of the Scillonians and his own family produced famous pilots down the years. His grandfather, known as 'Captain Ste', Stephen Jenkins, was the last skipper of the pilot cutter out of Scilly.

'My grandfather was born on Bryher in 1862, the son of a Trinity House pilot and his first job was looking after the Governor's pigs when he was 8 years old. When he left school he had a berth on a boat belonging to Captain Sherris, a respected sea captain, and he taught him navigation and seamanship and cargo work. You learned by doing the job in those days. In 1894 he bought up the old pilot cutter the *Agnes* and later converted her to carrying coal. He was the first door-to-door coalman on Scilly, supplying coal to the off islands and to the farmers who needed it for the glasshouses.

'It's hard to believe now but in his early days there were twenty-three pubs on St Mary's! They sold tobacco and spirits to visiting seamen (some of it smuggled) and much business, including pilotage, was carried out in the parlours of the pubs.

'St Mary's did manage better than the other off islands and for a long time they had a thriving boatbuilding business here. Boats of up to 100 tons were built in Hugh Town on Porthcressa beach, as well as the pilot gigs and cutters.' There has been something of a revival in the Scillonian gig, the fast rowing boats used by the pilots for years. As Alf says, they had to be fast as the system was that the 'first man aboard got the job.'

'Fishing, though, was never the business it was on the mainland. In the 1800s there was some Government money towards fishing and several large and expensive seine nets were shared among the islands. These nets were actually given names. I don't know what they were called on the off islands but those on Scilly were called Friendship, Habnab and Industry. But the freight charges here were always a killer — we couldn't compete with the ports on the mainland.'

However he has acquired much lore on the subject. The Jenkins family bought their crab pots from Sennen cove, on the mainland. These were made of withies.

'Some years ago an argument arose regarding the ownership of some pots found on board a fishing boat that came from a fishing port east of the Lizard. It became a bitter row with the fishermen being accused of hauling and pinching another man's gear. So, from that date, it was agreed that all pots made up by fishermen of the ports east of the Lizard would make their pots with the "binding" going round in a clockwise direction, while fishermen from ports west of the Lizard made their pots with the binding going anti-clockwise. Although few fishermen of today know this agreement, it is still traditional for their pots to be made in this fashion thinking their way is the correct way and not knowing the reason why.

'Scilly has miles and miles of soft sandy bottom which dries out leaving pools. The old Scillonians used to search the pools with a pitchfork and hundreds of fish were caught in this way. Winkles are still picked and eaten on Good Friday and although limpets were the staple diet of the old people in bygone times they aren't eaten much today.' In fact there are still mounds of limpet shells outside the ruined houses on Samson, evidence of their spartan diet.

'One method of fishing here must still be unique. That is the way the lighthouse keepers on the Bishop Rock catch their fish. They used a kite and a spinner — the kite is set off and left to go way down the wind. When far enough out it is left to fall into the sea and then slowly pulled back to the lighthouse. This is quite a successful way to catch mackerel and I have seen dozens of fish landed by the Bishop Kite.'

'Captain Ste' died in 1937 and his tradition of seafaring passed to his son, Bert, then to his grandson Alf. Captain Ste's last boat was the *Carmel*.

'Like Captain Ste she was old, but tough to the last. Built of pitch pine on oak and covered every year of her sixty odd years with coatings of tar, she was all but impossible to saw up. What couldn't be sawn was broken with a sledgehammer and what could not be broken had to go on the fire as it was. For several years each winter the living room fire would be lit and on would go one of these enormous long planks. They were so long that one end was in the fire and the other end out through the doorway into the front garden. Melting tar and pine resin stank out the house and was stopped from running back along the plank by keeping the other end higher, using the coal shovel on its end. Thus the family sat and froze until the plank burned through enough to close the front door.'

Alf is pessimistic about the future of the islands.

'I suppose you could say the tourist industry goes back about a hundred years but before the war it was usually quite wealthy people who came and stayed. There were more big hotels then – Holgate's, Springfield, as well as the Atlantic and Tregarthen's. (Holgate's and Tregarthen's were called after the skippers of boats who built them to cater for the tourists.) They didn't have launches to the off islands, they would charter a boat for a day or even for their whole stay and pay the boatman to take them where they wanted to go. There was one fellow who used to come and insist on going fishing with our family, even when it was pretty inconvenient, but before he left he would give every child in the family a suit of clothes.
'But look at it now! The kind of people who have moved in don't care. The sort of people who used to come up until a few

years ago used to come for the walking and the boating and
they'd be tired at night and go early to bed. Now it's discos
and barbecues until 2 a.m. Scilly is changing so fast.

'The beautiful beaches are covered in litter, it costs a fortune
to get here, and the local people are getting disillusioned and
moving out. Each industry here seems to have lasted about a
hundred years before it's gone bust — shipbuilding, fishing,
it'll happen to tourism too. What's left? Well, the flower
industry is nothing like it was. Too many farmers have found it
easier to put chalets on their land or let out cottages at £150 a
week than bother with the bulbs for the early flowers or with
early potatoes. Once upon a time just about every house
around here had a bit of land on which to grow vegetables for
the kitchen — they've all gone for building plots. Yet our
holiday season which used to run from Easter to October has
shrunk to July and August, like Newquay or Brighton, and
everyone's trying to make enough in eight weeks to live on.

'What the people who have come in here to live will do, I
don't know. They can't farm, most of them can't even row a
boat across the harbour, let alone make a living from the sea.
We sent six of our boys to the Falkland Islands with the Task
Force, to liberate other people's islands. When they come back
there'll be no homes and no jobs for them here. Nobody's
going to make sure they can continue to live their own lives on
their own islands, they're going to have to get off.'

At seventy-five, Alf's neighbour, Lily Trenear, is facing the
fact that she too might have to leave. For her, widowed and
with her pension and a few bed-and-breakfast visitors, living in
Scilly has become too expensive.

'One wouldn't wish the hard times back from the past but it
was a better place. It was hard though — we had the bakery
here and made all the bread. My father used to carry the water
from the well in the street with buckets on a yoke from his
shoulders and my mother would mix up 80 pounds of dough
by hand. It would be set to rise over night, then baked first
thing in the morning and we would all have to turn to helping
out before we went to school and after we got home at night.
People wouldn't be prepared to do that any more. You all

helped each other though. Now, it's very lonely. Nearly all the houses round me are empty all the winter and they used to be good family homes.

'The old people were looked after in their homes however hard times were. Now they go to Park House (the old people's home). It's very nice in there but it costs you £100 a week if you have any money or property. I'd do anything rather than go there, though. I went to see an old friend recently and she said they never go out, even in the lovely summer weather. Even though it's right on the beach the staff are too busy to bother walking with them down there or down the street as they are too slow. I think it was better a hundred years ago.'

At least the Scillonians are fortunate in having the unique pictorial record of life on their islands still held by the Gibsons. Alexander Gibson's photographs of wrecks have become, in recent years, world famous. The present Gibson, Frank, still takes photographs as well as running one of the handful of shops on St Mary's. The walls, from floor to ceiling, are covered with the photographs taken from the original plates belonging to his grandfather.

'We didn't start off as photographers. Our family had the first general store on Scilly, on the harbour where the new flats have been built. They sold just about everything from tins of meat to chandlery and God knows what. They also had the telegraph office, they morse-coded everything away. That was long before telephones, you see. Perhaps it was that which started him off but anyhow my great-grandfather got an interest in photography. I have pictures dating from 1869 so he might even have started before that but anyway it was at the very, very beginning of photography.

'But the leading light in the family was my grandfather, Alexander. Obviously from a very small boy he took a great interest and he built up the wreck pictures we have today. It's remarkable when you think he took all the pictures with a huge old plate camera. I have pictures obviously taken from boats, they couldn't have been taken in any other way, when the weather was truly terrible. There were only glass plates available then, of course, so they and all the gear had to be manhandled into the boats.

'The six-oared gigs were the boats of the day and so if there was a news story that was the way he got there — in a gig! There's a story how they came to him on Porthcressa beach one day and said there's a wreck on the Eastern Islands and how he ran down with all his gear to the boat. In those days a wreck was a *must* for all the islanders to see how much and what they could salvage. Of course my people were interested in the photography but sometimes old Alexander got there that quick he got the crews in the lifeboat being taken off the boat.'

Alexander's photographs of wrecks show the range of the ships sailing the seas around Scilly at that time — the big square-rigged grain ships from Australia, the nitrate carriers from South America, the mass of small sailing vessels plying along the coast. As Frank said,

'A sailing ship might be several months on passage and the duration of the voyage was so uncertain that owners could seldom establish markets for cargo in advance. It therefore became the practice for ships to leave foreign ports with no idea as to their eventual destination. They sailed with simple instruction to proceed to Falmouth for orders.'

As the date of arrival drew near the ship's owners would find the most profitable market for its cargo and pass instructions to Lloyds Signal Station which would relay them to the ship . . . the earliest means of signalling was by strings of flags and the ships often had to take a considerable risk when standing close in, to read the little squares of bunting.

The collection of photographs could have been much larger.

'We lost a lot of the plates. You see glass was very precious in those olden days on the islands and when they thought they'd finished with a particular series of plates they would clean them off and sell the glass. The flower growers were always wanting them for greenhouses. So a lot of the important stuff was sold off. They didn't put any importance to it.

'What we do have does show the changes in Scilly over that

period of time. The most obvious thing, of course, is the clothes and how they changed over the years but there was the appearance of the place and how that altered too. You can see the shipping in the harbour changing from the sailing ships and the rowing gigs to the first steamship right through to the present day.

'Some time in the 1870s the family found it very hard going to make a living, it was very hard times here then. It seemed to happen every so often that things would get particularly bad.'

Earlier in the century a letter from one of the off islands to the mainland summed it up.

'We, the undersigned inhabitants of the Scilly islands, humbly beg permission once more to lay before you, Sir, a statement of our distress praying that you will be prepated to use your influence on behalf of ourselves and starving families. In reply to the kind enquiry "what can be done for you?" permit us to say that we are in want of everything, and if some assistance be not afforded hunger will soon remove us to a situation where human help can be of no avail. Do not leave us to perish for lack of bread.'

In fact the period when Frank's family moved back temporarily to the mainland was when the bottom fell out of the boatbuilding industry and when the Scillonian pilots were no longer in demand for guiding sailing ships into port. From being a busy, thriving port with a harbour full of vessels, business fell away to nothing. J.G. Uren, who was postmaster of Penzance at the end of the nineteenth century, said in an essay,

'The result of all this, so far as Scilly is concerned, has been disastrous. If a whole pack of artillery were to bombard it, it would hardly find a ship as a target. One might draw a dragnet across Crow Sound without being able to fetch up as much as a length of chain cable − and were a typhoon to burst upon the islands − not a spar, not a chip could be found on which to wreak its fury. Scilly may yet serve to verify a reckoning, confirm a bearing or grace an entry in the log − but go near it!

– not while a shovel full of coal is left, or the screw can make one revolution.'

So the Gibson family set up as photographers in Penzance, while keeping their cottage on in Scilly. 'We stayed on until the 1930s and then my father came back. But all the time even then, if there was a wreck or anything, one of them would come back to the islands to take pictures, and they always kept somebody here in the summer because there was even then the beginnings of the tourist trade.'

'It was very small then. If you had fifty visitors in all the islands it was considered to be a lot. I remember reading in a book how Augustus Smith wrote to one of his friends complaining that the islands were so full of visitors it was dreadful – and he was talking about a few dozen, going through his gardens on the island of Tresco.

'The whole style of getting to the other islands was quite different in the old days. Visitors would go off in whole families, hiring a sailing boat and the owner for the day and being taken wherever they wanted to go and then he would bring them home in the evening. Everything was done under sail then between the islands, it was quite a different kind of tourism.

'Then as the boatbuilding finished so the flowers came along next. It was Richard Trevellick, here on St Mary's, who really started the early flower industry. The story is, and I believe it, that it was the sailors who started it, travelling from here to the Mediterranean and tropical countries. They would bring back bulbs and plants from foreign countries and scatter them under the walls and hedges so eventually Richard Trevellick spotted all these flowers growing wild and picked a few and sent them to Covent Garden and they fetched such an enormous price for the day that he there and then thought there must be money in cut flowers.

'It was Augustus Smith's son, Algernon, then, who developed the industry on proper lines. He went to Holland and saw how the flower industry was run there and came back with various varieties and put the industry on a firm footing. The most famous of course are the sols [soleil d'ors], the golden narcissus that are picked for Christmas.

'Now they are giving problems. I think with anything that is grown very intensively disease always sets in in the end and for years they've been plagued with eelworm and the only way they can deal with it is by treating them in boiling water — in a strictly controlled way — but what it does mean is that they have to lift all their bulbs every three years so it's a constant battle of re-planting and re-cycling all the time. Certainly the strength of the flowers is nowhere near what it was a hundred years ago — the strength of the stem, the colour, the scent, it's not as it was. Probably with overproduction they've bred out.

'Can you still make a living out of the flowers? Well there are good and bad years and some of them must or they wouldn't keep growing them. . . . It isn't what it was but the good years come when the rest of Britain is under freezing conditions so the 1981-82 winter was a good year for Scilly. Even at its best, though, the flower industry never created the work the old shipbuilding did — it really did make a lot of work for a lot of people here in Scilly and it almost vanished overnight and really hard times came to the islands for those who didn't grow flowers.

'But there's absolutely nothing at all here now for the young people — nothing, unless you can follow into a family business or a farm or have shares in a family boat. There's certainly no work and no housing either. The only area of freehold is this town and everybody's been selling out to the highest bidder. There's only mainlanders who've got such money. I have three daughters and only one of those three can stay behind. Even if I could support all three there'd be nowhere for them to live, no future for them.'

Frank feels the only hope for Scilly lies in going back to the one great natural resource, the sea, by developing the harbours and promoting them to yachtsmen from all over the world.

'It would mean employment, proper employment for a number of people, not just one person with a boarding house employing casual labour from the mainland in the summer. There are all the trades that go with harbours from boat designing, building and repairing, to engineering and sail-making and so on, and there could actually be apprenticeships for the young people over here.

'I keep harking back to the great days of Scillonian boatbuilding. There are so many sidelines to ships, it must create work for young people. On top of that many of these yachts actually want working crews and when you think back to the very old days then our Scillonian boys not only built the ships, they then went and crewed them, they travelled the world. I feel it's the only way, creating wealth for the community, not wealth just for one person making money for himself.'

Certainly there needs to be drastic action. Even getting to the islands is expensive. At 1982 prices it costs £42 to fly by helicopter and as the Department of Trade has pulled out of running the tiny airport, telling the islanders they must make it pay, there is a further £1.15p on each as each passenger lands. The newest ferry, in which most islanders have shares, has brought crushing interest charges and rocketting fuel prices, doubling the return fare from £12 in 1980 to £24 in 1982. Everything which is freighted in costs at least 10 per cent more than it would on the mainland and the expense of holiday homes and boarding houses, plus the ratchetting up of prices by those who came to the islands purely to make money, has resulted – at the time of writing – in a catastrophic falling off in the holiday trade.

The off islands have always had it even harder than St Mary's and their population is dwindling rapidly. In 1980 the school on Bryher closed. The population dropped from well over a hundred in the mid-1800s to less than fifty in 1982. On St Agnes, in 1980, there were six children at the primary school plus a 'follower'. (A follower is a child of 4-plus coming along.) St Martin's had only four children in its school. At 11 the children transfer to Britain's smallest comprehensive, that on St Mary's, where the off-island children become weekly boarders and live in a hostel.

At 16 they are encouraged to take up further education on the mainland; in fact their lives are geared to learning to leave the islands. The outlook for those wanting to return is bleak indeed. Teaching vacancies in the islands are few – the St

Agnes teacher is an exception, a St Agnes girl who trained and came back. A handful of others trickle back to work in the banks or solicitors' offices. But for those who do, housing is an insuperable problem unless they can get work for the Duchy of Cornwall and rent a Duchy house.

None of the older native islanders see a secure future in Scilly for tourism alone. Too many people have wanted expensive slices of the cake and their very size means that they cannot offer the facilities of a big holiday resort. The attempt to provide some of the amenities of modern holidaymaking drove many of the holidaymakers who were the backbone of the tourist trade and came for the peace, the walking and sailing to stay away. Others just cannot afford it.

Again and again older islanders mention Samson island, 'the one real bit of Scilly left.' The ruined walls of the Woodcocks' and Webbers' houses rise above the bramble and the bracken and only the seagulls are left to inhabit it. 'When you go to Samson,' said Frank Gibson,

'you can see all the history of Scilly in that little piece of land – the old graves of the oldest people, the walls and fields of those who came next, the houses of the Scillonians who made a living there just out of that tiny bit of land, the sea and by pilotage until it got too much for them. Then there was nothing and it has all gone back to the wild. If we ruin what is left in the islands just by people trying to make money and not caring about what's left, I can see the whole economy just collapsing and maybe the day will come when there'll be nobody left on Scilly at all.'

A couple of years ago a young islander returned to one of the off islands determined to make a financial go of things and make a living for himself. He failed. He committed suicide rather than go back to the mainland. One feels old Mrs Woodcock of Samson, she who was some kind of a witch, would have understood why.

PART 3

ON THE LAND

13

A farmer's wife

Edith Breedon

Edith Breedon was 93 when I spoke to her in 1982. She lives in a little cottage in the grounds of the farm she once farmed in North Warwickshire and from her sitting-room can see the garden she made 'out of a piece of woodland full of briars — but then I was only 70.'

'I remember my father once saying to me that he'd seen such changes in his lifetime, in the world and in England, that it was not possible there would ever be such a period of change again. He was alive when radio came but not to see men go to the moon. Recently I thought, my goodness, he didn't know what was ahead, what enormous changes would continue after he had gone. What a change there's been!

'I know that he told me that when he was a young man times were very hard up in the North — my parents came from the Lancashire/Cheshire border. There were still unmade-up roads and streets even in the towns. He saw the introduction of machinery on a large scale and the difference that meant to people when everything had previously been done by hand. He actually remembered the introduction of machinery into many of the mills in Lancashire. Of course, that put a lot of people out of work and took away a lot of skilled work from them. He said they used to sit in the streets and he said things got to such a pass that plants and weeds grew in the streets, actually grew up there where the roads should be.

'My father was apprenticed to an ironmaster in Manchester. At the same time the son of the owner of the Phoenix Iron works in Lewes was also apprenticed and they became friendly. When John (that was his name) finished his apprenticeship he went to work for his father, of course, in his iron works and he took my father and my uncle with him. Eventually my father became his manager so that's how we moved to Sussex.

'My earliest memories of my mother are of her mending. There were always two enormous baskets of clothes which required mending and you can see why when you think what we had to wear as children. I would wear a knitted vest, woollen combinations, a buttoned bodice, calico or flannelette drawers, a flannelette petticoat tied on with tapes and over all this a calico or flannelette petticoat fastened right up to the neck, and, of course, black woollen stockings.

'I can remember the volunteers going off to the Boer War and the popular song of the time, "Good Bye Dolly I must Leave You . . .". It's surprising how far you can go back. I asked my husband's grandfather when he was an old man what *his* father did and he said he kept the Hatter's Arms in Wharton. I asked him if he remembered what his grandfather did and he said, "indeed I do — he was a hatter."

'You see, the pub had been called the Hatter's Arms because it belonged to the son of the hatter. By this time I had taken it back to the great, great, great-grandfather and the time of the Napoleonic Wars. Those people were called Hull and they were quite important in North Warwickshire. Mr Hull the Hatter was also what you would call clerk to the council nowadays and he also was in charge of the village pound where they impounded stray animals.

'Anyway my parents sent me to train as a teacher. It wasn't what I wanted to do. I wanted to be a horticulturalist. My parents were quite forward in their outlook and they did enquire to see if I could do such a course. There were only two colleges where you could be trained in those days. One was for aristocrats to while away the time and the other one told my parents that I could go and be trained and they asked what possibility there was of an occupation for me afterwards and the answer was − a lemon. They just laughed. They said nobody could possibly employ a *woman* − it would be unheard of. So I was left with teaching.

'I trained in London and what a different place *that* was to nowadays. It was nice then and a wonderful place to be for the museums and art galleries and, most of all, the theatre. If you had half a crown you could go into the middle of London on a tram and the underground, buy a seat in a theatre and have tea afterwards and go back again and all for that half a crown. I saw all the great performances of Henry Irving and Ellen Terry.

'But afterwards I found it very hard to find a job and the men always had the priority. Finally I found one in Hampshire and was very happy but then my sister, who was also teaching, said there was a vacancy at her school in Warwickshire and my parents thought it would be good for us to live together. However I was not accepted as the school committee said it was not its practice to engage sisters. However the county education committee kept my application and they later wrote to me and offered me a job at Wood End School quite near here so I have lived in Warwickshire and this part of Warwickshire for over seventy years − a lifetime.

'I was offered the princely sum of £80 a year, a £10 rise on my previous job. We always lived in digs in those days of course and they cost me 12s. 6d. a week, full board. That doesn't sound much but out of £80 a year it meant nearly half of what I earned went on the digs. It didn't leave you much and you certainly weren't well off but it was amazing what we did on it. We played tennis and rode on bicycles and went to village hops. I remember being upset when I was invited to a posh ball and I couldn't go because I just couldn't afford the right kind of dress. There was no question of having money for things like evening dresses. I used to make some of my clothes but I was never very keen or satisfied with the results but there was always a village dressmaker who would make you a dress for a couple of shillings.'

In 1913 Edith married her husband, Jack, a farmer.

'We've had several farms. The first was at Curdworth, then we went to Dunton and then here, to Black Greaves. So I've lived in three places in the seventy years or so, all on the Kingsbury Road and all on the same side of it.

'It's changed so much. Not only the way of life but the countryside has changed. Every time you go out now there's another hedge gone. For years it hadn't altered much but now there's just great big enormous fields because of all the mechanisation. When we first started there was hardly any machinery. Everything was done just as it had been done in Warwickshire and, indeed in England, for centuries. I remember the very first tractor in this part of the world and it wasn't a bit like tractors are today – it seemed marvellous to us at the time.

'Of course we didn't have a car, we had a wagon, and all the ploughing was done with horses. Things were so very different. We had only a medium-sized farm but we had to employ a ploughman, a waggoner, a couple of labourers and a girl in the house.

'Now farming is all specialised but it was proper mixed farming in those days. You grew crops of all kinds but you also kept cows, pigs, sheep, hens, ducks, geese, even guinea fowl – a real mixed farm. All the milking was done by hand, naturally. I didn't much like milking and really did very little after I was married. I looked after all the birds, bringing chickens and ducklings up in incubators for sale.

'It was a very busy life, always some work waiting to be done, there was plenty of work and plenty of cooking. In those days there were absolutely no conveniences. All the water had to be pumped up in the yard, by hand, brought into the house, heated over the range and carried upstairs if you wanted a bath. Fortunately we did have a bath and the water did run away from it but it was still a performance getting the water up there. All the water had to be pumped too for the stock, for the washing, everything. It was hard, very hard. People don't realise today just how much water gets used. Of course there were no flush toilets.

'Life is not only very different now – it's very luxurious and very easy but I shouldn't think it's as satisfying. On the whole life seemed much happier then. People looked happy and they don't look happy any more. They don't realise how lucky they are to live in such a luxurious time. We had nothing comparatively, not even electricity.

'I heard one of those radio programmes recently where the people on it were asked if they were put back, say, one hundred years what would they miss most? Not one of them said electricity. They said radio and television and all those luxury items but nobody said electricity because they simply couldn't imagine being without it. To them now, our life would seem like life in the raw.

'The oil lamps had to be done every day. They had to be filled and then the glasses both cleaned and polished and the wicks trimmed. All the knives had to be cleaned and sharpened every day on the block. Oh, we'd no time to be bored. I think people are bored nowadays and that's why they get into mischief.

'The farmworkers worked very hard when it was all done by hand. When you watched them cutting the hay it was beautiful to see. The children just loved the haymaking. They played around the haycocks and picked the flowers and chased off rabbits – you can't imagine it now with all the big machines. There were no chemical sprays, no artificial fertilisers – just good old manure from the farmyard which had to be spread by hand.

'Then at harvest there came the thrashing machine and that was a really big excitement. They came around all the farms in turn and charged so much but if you gave the men a dinner they charged less. In those days the house was always full of people and you never knew just how many you would be cooking for or who would sit down to dinner.

'You always gave them something substantial. Meat then was cheap and easy, you'd cook a joint like a leg of mutton, topside or sirloin and you always gave everyone a good cut off the joint. Then we always grew all our own vegetables so there were plenty of those. That would be followed by a big pudding, a steamed one or a pastry of some kind.'

Edith's interest in history, both family and local, has made her record it in a book on which she is now working 'though it might be thought crazy at my age. . . .'

'The people of North Warwickshire have tended to be overlooked. When you think of Warwickshire you think of the south – Shakespeare country, Warwick, Kenilworth – yet this part of the country has produced its own writers, explorers, a famous botanist. When I came here the local people knew every tiny village but nowadays those who live here don't seem to have heard of half the places, even those around them. I say, "do you know Elscote and Ansley", and they say, "no, where are they?" It's become a bigger world. In fact there are some village names which aren't even known any more, they've just disappeared.

'The traditions are going too, very quickly. Do you know the first battle of the Civil War was fought at Curdworth two miles away? It was only a scuffle between the Roundheads and Cavaliers but it was the very first time they'd met. The Cavaliers were bringing armaments from Kenilworth Castle so they couldn't travel very quickly and the Roundheads set on them and hampered them until at last they made a stand at Curdworth and had a little battle and killed some of them. Then they went off and fought Edgehill in the south of the county, the first real battle of the Civil War.

'We've always been at the crossroads here, in the middle of England. We had the coal pits here and some manufacturing but it's always been rich, rich farming land and that's what it's been most valuable for. Mind you, there were more pits when I first came here. Kingsbury was flourishing and working well and they'd reopened Baxterley or Baddesley as it's sometimes called. There were still plenty of people who remembered the great disaster. When we were first married we used to fetch our coal from either Kingsbury or Baxterley in the wagon. Baxterley was the better coal. It was only a few shillings then for a whole cartload.'

Black Greaves farm lies near the oddly named Bodymoor Heath.

'It used to be called Hemlingford Green. Nobody knows why it changed but they did have a big tussle up there a great while ago, I think about seven or eight years before I was born. Anyway sometime about a hundred years ago some prizefighters came from Birmingham to have a great bare knuckle fight there and men came from as far as the Black Country, Stafford and Stoke, to see this big fight. It was widely advertised.

'Now at that time Lord Norton lived at Ham Hall and, being the Lord of the Manor he was responsible — or thought he was — for the morals of the village and he wasn't going to have any prize fight that would lead to trouble and bad language. So he found out when they were coming and got the parson and some of his own men and out they went and stopped the wagon bringing the prizefighters into the village and sent them back. Of course trouble broke out, especially from those who'd come a long distance to see the fight. They were furious. So instead of having a prize fight, Lord Norton had a real battle and some were hurt but I don't think anyone was killed. That's the only story I know about the place but it's not a nice name, is it?

'I started looking into my husband's family, the Breedons. They originated in the Baxterley area and I found an old book in which it said that the Dugdales and the Breedons were the principle landowners so they must once have been very well off. They are buried in Baxterley churchyard in some of the oldest graves in this part of the county. I have a sampler worked by one who died two hundred years ago. The Breedon line is like those of the great aristocratic houses, it goes straight back. They have never moved out of this area. They really know the farming here. We had my son christened at Baxterley church near his ancestors.

'By a coincidence the church magazine in which his christening was recorded contained a page from old parish records transcribed by a visiting parson. Baxterly used to come in Grendon parish. One of the entries said, "On this day was buried Mary Breedon. She was buried in this parish by her two sons, John and William, not in the churchyard, she having been excommunicated." I was so intrigued I asked our parson and he said don't worry, they could be excommunicated then for not going to church and it was probably for that. Perhaps he was right. It was all a long time ago, in the 1600s, but they obviously couldn't bury her properly as she had been excommunicated.

'But we go back farther than that. I saw a note in another book which said the farm of Black Greaves used to belong to Lord Middleton and it gave a place name. I've never been any good at geography and I didn't know where it was but I told a friend and she said she knew; it was in Worcestershire. Not only that but her husband's family came from that very place. Lord Middleton had owned land around here too — there's a village called Middleton nearby.

'So I went off and I've actually got copies of the old deeds and they go back a tremendous way, to the early 1300s. It's strange that the only two farms mentioned in Dugdale's *Antiquities of Warwickshire* are Dunton and Black Greaves and I've lived in both. I've a theory about the name. Greaves are a part of armour and perhaps people were recognised by different bits of armour they wore, gauntlets, helmets and so on, and we were the people with the black greaves.

'Of course Black Greaves farmhouse now isn't that old. There's a Tudor part of the house at the back but the front is Georgian so there must have been at least one older building on the same site.'

Edith can look back on a life spanning nearly a century. She wonders now about farming skills.

'They're no longer close to the earth any more. They're separated from the earth by the wheel, by the machine. They're apart from it. They've learned new skills, of course: mechanical skills. But they used to be able to do so much, they knew so much. It's going so fast now there's hardly the memory of it left.'

14

The little old boys

George Crisp — farmworker

Mr Crisp sits in his immaculate cottage at Ditchingham, just half a mile or so over the Suffolk border into Norfolk. In the next room his wife lies in bed, helpless from the effects of a stroke. Looking after her takes up nearly all his time.

He came from a family of fishermen,

'but I never did want to go to sea. It never appealed. My old dad, he never put no sea into me.

'I came to this house a married man and I've lived here for fifty-one years. When I come there wasn't a house in sight — they've all been built since I've been here.

'Changes, changes — what changes. . . . Blimey, when I first started off I worked seven days a week for 6s. My very first job at 14 was cleaning the beet [sugar beet] by hand. Every beet had to be topped and tailed and cleaned by hand and then grinded by hand. The differences I've seen over the years. . . . We used to work even by night then with an old oil lamp, for you see when I first started off it were Christmas time.

'Then as well as cleaning the beet I used to look after the chickens and the pigs, mix up the pigswill in the tub. Those old farm workers then, they thought they was wonderful. When you were a boy you daren't say nothing to them —

they'd a-killed you. I used to work with this old boy cleaning
the beet, throwing them in the heap to go into the grinder.
Well, there was a dealer used to come around the farms in a
horse and cart and he'd come and buy up calves and so on. If I
held his pony for him he used to give me 6d. As soon as I
heard a pony and cart come in as I was cleaning the beet, then
out I'd go to see if it were that old dealer and earn my 6d. but
one time I did it and it was another old boy and I didn't know
him so I went back and when I got back old Will he said to me,
"you've been a-buggering about out there again and missed
cleaning two old beets." He was only an old farm worker but
that was how they were, they'd dominate you.

'Another of my first jobs was to take the horses down into
the fields for the binder. Take three down, bring three back,
that was how it was in harvest time. After I'd been on the farm
a good while I took all the horses over but in those first days
everything was done by hand and horse. I used to cut the hay
with horses, two of them, then there were three on the binder.
All the hoeing, five rows at a time, was done by horses. It was
backwards and forwards, backwards and forwards all day.
When I first started in the spring of that year, it was leading
the horses on the horse hoes in the fields. They used to walk
your legs off. Those old farmworkers used to work like the
very devil. I'd work with this chap and he didn't stand for
nothing. They didn't loiter about like they do now. Well this
old boy said to me when my poor old legs was nearly dropping
off — he used to count the rounds up and down, up and
down, looking at his watch all the time — "it's near on half-
past five just another two rounds, my lad, and then we'll pack
up." Cor blimey, I went like the very devil then and when
we'd done the two rounds he'd say, "look, we've just got time
for another. . . ."

'Then there was the old thrashing machine. When you
worked on the farm you hated the sight of them coming on
and wish they'd go away quick as it was the dirtiest job, you
know. You'd get covered with chaff and dust and the stacks
were full of rats and mice. One of my jobs when I got to be
horseman and had to go to work at five in the morning to see
to my horses, was to look after the thrashing machine and
knock the top off so the thrashing man didn't have to come so

early. I used to get steam up for him. They used to have a pan go on top of the chimney over night. Then they'd bank down the fire, shut it down and put the cap on so in the morning I'd knock the cap off, stoke up again so that when the thrashing man come there'd be 20 or 30 pounds of steam on. I didn't get nothing for that. In the wintertimes some of the old chaps without work used to tramp about behind the thrashing machine. There'd be perhaps twenty stacks on a farm and these old men'd come and look after the chaff and corn and there'd be work then all winter. They were called tramp thrashers. They used to pay five shillings a day for local labour on the thrashing but the tramp thrashers'd get sixpence a day extra. Now the only time you see those old machines is on show days.

'We had to be able to do it all. I could scythe — they used to scythe all round the field edges then. I drove a racking machine — not many can remember them, just old bygones they are now. I drove an old sailing reaper, then the horse binder. Those old boys used to follow behind tying up all the sheaves behind the reaper — nowadays they come in a field with a combine and it's cut, carted and gone in a couple of hours.

'Then thatching was another job I learned. There's no one left I reckon now who could stack a stack and thatch it like I could. The last farm I worked on, I stacked twenty-one stacks and thatched them all — this was corn thatching with wheat straw. It's a dying trade. It's all baled now, even hay. I don't believe you could find anyone around here who even knew how to stack.

'When I got married I looked after all the horses. I loved horses. I worked seven days a week for 30s. and I got another 9d. for being a foreman with eight or nine men under me. We'd a hard time, mind, but the wife was a marvellous manager. She'd write a book out for 6s. of groceries and then cross half of them off if she'd not the money to pay for them that week. That's what's so sad now her being like she is. We was having a lovely time with enough money to get about when this had to happen. I worked fifty-one years and never had a day off sick apart from the time I got metal in my eyes and was blinded until they was put right.

'It isn't just what you remember. They did seem happy in the old days. People worked together and were happy. All they do now is grumble about how much they can get for how little they can do. At that time of day they'd see how much they could do and how good they could do it too.

'I remember one old boy in the days when they used to brag about carrying corn up to the granary. Well this little old boy, he had a bet. They bet him he couldn't carry a comb of beans up the granary steps. ["Comb" is pronounced "coom".] That was 20 stone. So they betted him sixpence he couldn't do it. He'd be all of 60 years old. Anyway he carried this comb up into the granary, ten or fifteen steps up, to get his 6d. then he brought it down again. Dammit, they say, why you brought that old comb back down and he said I didn't carry it up there for nothing. He'd won his 6d. but brought the comb down. Everything was measured in combs then – oats was 12 stone, barley was 16, wheat was 18 and beans was 20. That was the size of the sack, a comb sack, and they varied in weight because they held different amounts. The heavier the crop was, the more you could get into a bag, so oats was light and beans was heavy. Think what we used to hump about!

'The women worked too, in the dairy, grinding and cleaning beet, milking cows, cleaning out the cowsheds and in the fields, carrot singling. All that for 1s. a day so you can see how it's changed in my lifetime.

'There was no dole then either. A lot of the old boys in the old days'd go and work in the stone pit when there wasn't no work. 12s. a week they got for getting the stone out and sifting it to go on the roads to fill up the potholes. There wasn't no tar on these country roads then. All the roads were done by clay and stones and bricks, stones from the pit – hoggen they called it. They used to put the hoggen down and then chuck the clay on the top and that was how all these little old by-roads were made.

'What's gone too is all the old characters. There was some funny little old boys around here times past. You ever heard of that book by Miss Lilias Rider Haggard, *I Walk by Night*? I knew that old poacher right well – old Rolf. He used to go out at three or four in the morning and shoot half a dozen pheasants and be out selling them in Bungay by eight o'clock. He were a proper poacher, you see. They called him the King of the Norfolk Poachers and he could kill twelve pheasants in one night without moving from the one spot. Then he'd be hoeing the old beet during the day.

'He was working with me when I was a lad and there was another lad with us who had twenty or thirty warts on his hand. We was a-hoeing at the time and old Rolf he did say, "I'll charm them away, I'll buy them off you. So count them up, count how many there is and make sure that's all", and then he gave him tuppence for them, cos he had bought them, him being a charmer you see.

'He'd brought along an old copy book he'd been writing in and he lent it to that young lad and he took it home to his mother. Then one day Miss Lilias come there and the mother said to her, "what you think of that old Rolf, he did charm my old boy's warts", and Miss Lilias she did say that was poppycock. Then the woman said, "and he gave my boy an old copy book too", and by God, Miss Lilias didn't think as that was poppycock and she said, "can I have a look at it?" and the mother said, "it's in the old drawer here" — she'd chucked it in there. So she got it out and Miss Lilias looked at it and she was down to old Rolf's in about ten minutes and that's how the book came about, the story about him.

'Did the warts go away? Oh yes, they went away. Perhaps they'd a-gone anyway but they went. I've done it myself since, scores of times. There's one girl lives at Diss now, I charmed her warts. When I got to contracting out on my own I was on her farm one day cutting the hay and this little girl Brenda was in the house. I was having a cup of tea and her mother said that poor Brenda's hands was full of warts so I said count them and I'll buy them off you. She'd sixteen or twenty. Well I never thought no more about it but when I saw her mother next time she said, "my word, but them warts has all gone — you're a wonderful man!" I do think you just buy the warts and then they do go. I still see the girl and she still remembers it, she's a woman now with children of her own.

'Another old character around here was old George Baldry. He used to have boats on the river he'd built himself and hire them out on the Waveney. After he got married he had a little stall on the riverside selling teas. Fifty years he courted that woman! Her father was a builder, you see, and he felt old George and his boats weren't good enough for her and her parents made her promise she wouldn't marry him in their lifetime so old George waited until they died and married her then.

'He was a great inventor, old George. He tried to make a perpetual motion [machine] for years and years. I went to see him one day with an old man. I was only a boy and he took him in to see where this perpetual motion was but he said don't let that boy come in, these young 'uns might copy it. He'd tried for so many years. He got it to go once for about ten or fifteen minutes I heard. I think it was a kind of wheel that you weighted and it just kept a-going. He was an eccentric old boy. I remember talking to his wife when they'd been married some time and must have been going on 70. They'd been to some do in Bungay and I asked if she'd enjoyed it and she said "George kept me out till all of eleven o'clock and when we come home he still wanted to go to Norwich . . ." — that did have a special meaning then for you-know-what.

'I've lived all my life in Ditchingham apart from travelling around showing shire horses. Ditchingham used to be one of the biggest populated villages in Norfolk, perhaps the biggest. You see in the old days all the farms around here employed fourteen or fifteen men. Now there's only four or five on 6000 acres. There's no one at this next farm here now and there used to be fourteen men when old man Cooke had it. He'd employ anybody. Then up the hill there was another fourteen men — cowmen, horsemen, labourers — now there's three on that farm.

'That's how farming is run nowadays with this here mechanisation and big business farming. They make all the farms into one, make huge fields and cut down the trees and get rid of the hedges. The big estates have taken over.

'Every time one of these farmers, who have been farming these farms for generations, dies then the estate moves in. Brigadier Carr's estate, that is, he do buy them up and they all get run as one big business by Saville's, the estate agents. There's six good-sized farms around here all gone into that one big business. It don't seem to have much to do with farming no more.'

15

In service — the poacher's wife

Mrs Lill Digweed lives in a tiny cottage overlooking the village green at Stretton-on-the-Fosse in the Cotswolds. Stretton is, itself, a very small village hidden in a deep valley between rolling hills. Most of the cottages are Cotswold stone, as is the church, and there is a small amount of new building. But the village has changed out of all recognition, says Lill. 'There's not so many real villagers now, too many townspeople coming in and doing up the places.'

There is a theory that most of the villagers are called Digweed and directly related to Lill. The rest, said one old man, Sid, 'are called White and them was on her Father's side. . . .' His family went back a while too, in the nearby village of Campden, providing generations of publicans.

'There was seven pubs in Campden until the First War when the parson and the squire's wife got together to get some of them closed down. In those days they'd be open from six in the morning, for the labourers, until eleven at night. My dad came back from the war to find his pub had been shut up and his livelihood gone until he could get another. When he moved out he found a couple of accounts stuck away in a cupboard dating from the 1650s, that must have been back near enough to the Religious Wars.'

Lill's cottage sitting-room shines from floor to ceiling with polished brass. A kettle permanently sings on the hob of the old stove in the big open fireplace and on a fine day she sits at her door and watches the world go by.

Almost the whole of Lill's long life has been spent in Stretton.

'I was brought to Stretton when I was a fortnight old. My mother had just had me. It was over eighty years ago and we came in a cart belonging to a Mr Longford and lived up the village in some houses which aren't lived in any more.

'My dad worked on the land. He was a tree feller. It was just so different then. All round the village there was big houses, like the Manor up the top, and farms, and there wasn't no unemployment then, everyone worked out on the land. You see they needed the labour, they didn't have all those machines and implements. The machines came in and the men got less and less. I hope I won't live to see it but perhaps there'll come a time when everything gets done by machine and there's no work for people any more.

'They even have machines for sheep shearing now, don't they? When I was young the shearers'd come and perhaps shear twenty sheep in a day and think they'd done well. Now it's two hundred. But me Dad was kept in work, you see, and he'd quite a family, seven of us.

'My mother now, she was a midwife, she delivered all the babies around here and in the village. She was never qualified mind you, many of them weren't in them days, but she was really very clever at it. She was always spotlessly clean and wore starched white aprons and so on. The women around really trusted her and would always call her in. It wasn't just working women either, there was Mrs Courage who lived in the big house up the top and she asked my mother if she'd come in when she was took bad. My mother said she wasn't sure, she'd just had a baby herself and there was a pile of little ones back home but when the lady's time came she had my mother in and then paid her for two weeks to look after her.

'I went to the village school – and there were many more children then – and really and truthfully those were the happiest days of my life, the only time in my whole life when I didn't have to work hard. It didn't last long though as of course I had to leave when I was 14 and then I went straight into service.

'My first place was in Stratford in a big tall house near the hospital. It was to a young couple, I think they'd only been married about a month. I went as a "general" – that means I did absolutely everything, all the cooking, all the cleaning, all the housework, lighting fires, boiling water, all of it and at just 14 years old. I was pretty homesick at first of course but it wore off and they were good to me and I got on well with them. I can't remember now what I got paid but it was very, very little – just a few pounds for the whole year for doing everything.'

After a short break Lill went off to Birmingham, as far away as she was ever to go.

'Now they was grander. The man was a businessman and he'd one arm. I think he lost the other in the war. He'd a wife and two children, a son and the daughter and the daughter was so helpless she couldn't even boil an egg or lift a kettle. She'd never had to do anything, you see. I had to wear a uniform there, a print frock and a starched apron and a cap in the mornings and a black dress, a frilly apron, collar and cuffs and a lace hat in the afternoons. They were very strict about my getting washed and changed. They weren't bad to me though, treated me quite well, although I had to take all my meals separate-like in the kitchen. Well, I'd been with them a year or two when the husband began spending more and more time at his business and it turned out he was carrying on with someone else.

'My mistress, she poisoned herself. She killed herself dead. I'd missed her from the house and wondered where she was and went looking for her. They were well off enough to have a car and there she was in the front of it, stretched out over the front seat. I didn't know whatever to do. Then I got myself together and as they did have a telephone – which was pretty uncommon then – I phoned the doctor and the police and they come.

'I was written about in the *News of the World* because I'd found her, see. I didn't stay long after that. I waited on until she'd been laid to rest and for a week or two after but I didn't want to stay there without her. She'd been a good mistress to me and I thought it was wrong what happened to her. Her daughter was just as different, a real hoity-toity so-and-so.

'That was the trouble with service you see. It was all right to a certain extent but you'd not any choice if you were a girl – just service or on the land. If you were lucky and got a good home then that was all right but a lot of them were real hoity buggers who felt they could treat you how they wanted.'

After seven or eight years of 'walking out' with a young man from the village Lill married her husband, George.

'I'd nine children, six girls and three boys, and eight of them survived. One little girl died a little while after she was born but then many did in those days. My husband he started out working on the land and then went to be a shoemaker in Moreton. He made lovely shoes, really beautiful they were but there wasn't ever enough work. He did all kinds of things but he still used to get out of work as they stopped employing people on the land.

'We used to live up in those same houses at the top where my parents used to live and there was three of the men and they used to go poaching. Now they were really good at that. They'd work by night, as you might say. They'd come back with chickens and rabbits, even taties and sprouts. I suppose you'd have to call it pinching but we didn't really see it like that. I was frightened to death. I used to have to sit up and wait for him with a hot drink and I'd worry and think surely the coppers'll get you, sure as God made little apples, but he never did get caught. He was a terror. His hobby was keeping canaries.

'I'll tell you another story too. We'd nothing to eat in the house at all one day and there was this big cockerel used to come in the garden – we'd a lovely bit of garden. Well one day he came in and we were all that hungry I thought, "I'll have you, mate" and I got a bit of corn and I enticed him in and then I got him into the pantry and I picked up the chopper and I chopped his bloody head clean off! Just as I did it there comes a tapping on the door and I was that frightened I could hardly move. It was the lady from the big house across the road and it was her cockerel. So I shut the larder door and went and said, "What can I do for you Miss C?" and it turned out she wanted my husband to do some odd jobs, she wasn't looking for her cockerel at all. I've often laughed about it since. But he made a really good meal for us he did.

'To help out I'd go pea-picking, potato-picking, strawberry-picking, pushing the kids in the pram. I'd be up by six cutting up sandwiches and putting tea in flasks and then off we'd go. Usually they'd give you a lift home at the end of the day and on the back of a lorry.

'I've had a hard life and then I was poor, really poor. I've known when I hadn't a penny piece to my name nor a crust of bread in the larder and there was many like that then. But I never owed anybody anything. My children never had much either. They all went to Sunday school and on a Saturday night I'd wash, starch, iron and air all their clothes clean for the morning and I'd send them all off to Sunday school looking like little ladies and gentlemen. I've always had to work hard but it was very, very, very hard when all the children was little step-and-steps.

'But the village was a different world. There was a carrier at the bottom end, he'd bring shopping back for you or take you into Shipston. There was a shop next door, one over the road, two shops and a post office down the hill. Now there's nothing at all. There's one bus of a Saturday which takes you to Shipston at ten o'clock and comes back at eleven thirty so you've no time and another on a Tuesday afternoon for the market at Moreton. You can't get out now like you could sixty years back. The people who have come in to live have cars but they never think of offering you a lift. In the days when folk had horses and carts they'd ask you.

'They live in the houses and drive off and work somewhere else and they don't mix in with the people who have lived here all along. In the old days if you were sick, or old, or had a baby then the people would come along and help out. Now it's the old people's home or the hospital or the home help. The parents don't seem interested. At least I'd a good father and mother even though my Dad did like his drink but then most men do. He made rhubarb wine and parsnip wine and had apples crushed to make cider. He made barrels and barrels of cider.'

When her children had grown up a bit, Lill went and cooked at one of the big local houses, for Sir George and Lady Gordon-Lennox.

'I cooked for them for twenty-one years, in fact I can say I cooked for the Queen of England. Their eldest son was at Sandhurst and won the sword of honour and they threw a big party for him up in London and I did a lot of the food. I made some cheese straws for it and apparently the Queen had some and she sent a message through Lady Gordon-Lennox to tell me they were beautiful. After that I was always being asked to make cheese straws for everyone and in the end I got fed up with it.'

The Gordon-Lennoxes eventually sold up nearly all their property and went to live in Scotland but Lill's tiny cottage is still owned by the family and she can live in it for as long as she wants.

Now she keeps busy in her little house and around the village. I was told she still went in for some of the races in the summer fête, given a slight start.

'I suppose I'm proof that hard work never hurt no one. I've been blessed with good health until recently. Sometimes I get down in the dumps though. With my husband gone now and so many of my friends there's not much left of the old times. You may not get as hard up now as we used to but I don't think the times are all that good. You still have to manage on your bit of pension but in the old days you were all hard up together. Now nobody bothers any more.'

16

The Dartmoor man

Jack Down now lives in the little village of Keinton Mandeville in Somerset. His smallholding lies down a winding lane and although now into his mid-seventies he is still hale and hearty and busy, working his land and also doing some work for the local undertaker. In the kitchen his wife, Jane, boiled Devon apple dumplings on the stove. It is a second marriage for both of them and as well as long-grown-up children they have two teenage daughters, both of whom were doing their homework on the kitchen table. 'Our eldest girl was born when Jack was 59,' Jane said with pride. Dozens of rosettes, prizes she has won with her pony, festoon the kitchen walls.

Beside a log fire in his sitting room, Jack reminisced about his early life, spent on Dartmoor.

'I knew just about every inch of Dartmoor, I rode it all the time and in all weathers.

'I was born in 1908 when my father was a farmer at Manor Farm, Cudliptown. I lived there until 1921 when we moved to Brympts Farm at Dartmeet. Father only had a small farm at Cudliptown, about 63 acres, but he was Moor Man for the West Quarter of Dartmoor. He used to rent 25,000 acres off the Duchy of Cornwall for £25 a year. Then he let the land out, you see, to farmers from down Tavistock, Gunnislake, Lamerton and all that. They used to send their sheep out during the

summer and in they days it used to be two bob a score for
sheep and a shilling for a score of lambs. They run them on the
moor from when they sheared them in June until the end of
September. This was so that farmers in what we called the in-
country had time to cut their grass and make their hay because
their stock was up on the moor. Bullocks was ten bob a score.

'I can just about remember back until I was about 4. I hadn't
started school. My mother's father and mother, they lived just
above us and the Reverend Baring-Gould, William Crossley
and Robert Bernard, they used to stop up at Granfer's during
the week. The Reverend was the preacher over to Lew-
trenchard. They used to go up on the moors where all they old
crosses and hut circles and all that are, and go up looking for
relics. What I can remember was getting a hiding. My gran
used to give me an orange and she'd take a knife and cut the
orange across and put a lump of sugar in the orange. Well, the
Reverend he gave me an orange and I sucked it and said to he,
"you haven't put no lump of sugar in the bugger. . . ." Of
course he told mother and my mother gave me a real big
hiding.

'All our life was spent with the sheep then. Father, he had to
see to the dipping too. The last really big dipping we did was
in 1920 after they'd brought in the dipping law in 1918. The
moor had to be cleared on a Saturday and it always had to be
done the nearest weekend to the 15 of July. Us used to start on
the Friday, me and father — me only a boy then — riding up
with some good collie dogs and start and round the whole lot
up. On the Saturday the farmers would come — perhaps as
many as forty farmers — from all over the place and they'd
come up on the moor and pick out their sheep because the
police would ride up on the moor on the Sunday to see if there
were any sheep about and if they still found any up there then
my father, as Moor Man, would be in blinking trouble. Father
had a big sheep dip put in which took fifteen or twenty sheep
at a time and all the farmers would get together and dip the
sheep, sending up one or two men to make sure there were no
more on the moor.

'There was a place about half a mile away where the water
come out over a high hedge down a steep drop. Well, we had
horses and carts full of cider barrels and they had a biggish

hole in the top. We'd bend a piece of old galvanised metal around the water to make a shoot and back up the carts under it and in three minutes the barrel would be full and it would be taken back to the dipping. We'd horses and carts going there and back all day and there was one chap did nothing else but mix the dip. Cooper's dip powder they used in those days. He'd mix it in a bucket with a stick to get all the lumps out.

'My family originated from Par in Cornwall, then they moved to Ashwater and then to Peter Tavy. Then Granfer and his brother Tom they went off to Australia, that must have been in the mid 1800s. Granfer told me that as they walked out of the door to walk to Plymouth to get the boat his father said, "they foreign hills are green and when you get there, there'll be nothing to be seen!" — he remembers that as the last words he ever said to him. He went steerage from Plymouth but my Granfer didn't like it and come home. He only stopped there above eighteen months. He said, "durn it, when they shear the sheep they just smack it off anyhow", and Granfer were used to doing a tidy job, see. Anyway his brother Tom he left Australia at the same time and he went to Auckland in New Zealand and he went off somewhere wild and had a butcher's shop and never came back but he sent his son to be educated at Oxford and *he* never went back to New Zealand.

'Then father ended up at Cudliptown. Of course we'd no modern amenities when I was a lad. No electric or anything, just oil lamps and candles — we nearly caught the house afire once. We had this new kind of a petrol pump-up lamp with a mantle to it — like a Tilley lamp but using petrol not paraffin. It was supposed to give 400 candlepower and it gave a beautiful strong light. So we pumped it up and put it on the table and, darn it, it caught fire. We'd big sash windows and I pushed one up and picked up the lamp and threw it out on to the moor. There was a big flash and that was it. We never had one no more.

'I left school at 13 and helped father with the sheep. I wanted to shear too. For six weeks there'd be nothing else but sheep shearing and gangs of men would go around from one farm to another shearing. It was all hand shearing then, of course. It was at old Frank Morison's that I started shearing. Father used to go out and I'd want to go with him and he used to say to the farmers, "my lad'll come and do some shearing", and the farmers would say, "we need to get on with it and don't want no youngsters and that." I'd sheared our own sheep though. Anyway they went up to Frank Morison's and come the end of the week he said to the men, "you fellows aren't going to finish my sheep today are you?" and father says no. Frank said, "I want 'un finished" so father says, "bestways you send home after Jack." So his daughter come riding out to fetch me and I come out on the shearing. So I sheared there and Letterdale, whose farm we was going on to next day, he was there and he turned round and said, "right, lad, you come and do some shearing for me." Five bob a score I got in they days. I used to do forty-five a day, ten bob a day, very good money then especially for a boy of 14. I don't know what I did with it though − spent it, I suppose.

'Then father gave it up and we moved to Dartmeet. He didn't keep on as Moor Man. A farmer friend had got killed and he'd two boys left so father handed it over to they to do. We still ran some of our own sheep on the moors though and we'd be up riding out weekends to see if they was all right or to see if the bullocks got in a bog and help them out. There's a lot of bad bogs on Dartmoor.

'There was one case of a farmer called George Giles. He lived down near Tavistock and he come out one Saturday to see his sheep. It was a funny thing with these sheep from the different farms. They would all run in their own part of the moor. Where you put them, there they'd stop. One lot might stop here, another lot you'd find the other side of Lydford and some would be right over as far as Buckfastleigh. This farmer was at a place called Spittle Bottom and he rode right into a bog and his horse couldn't get out. He couldn't get 'un out and he got down and kept fighting but he daren't leave the horse. Come eleven o'clock at night, his son come out to father and said have you seen my father and he said we ain't, but he'd knew he'd gone up the Moor on this young horse, so we got some lanterns and father called me out of bed and off we went. We'd done a good three or four miles when old Giles, he sees the light and he starts a-hollerin' and he kept shouting and us went towards him. Darn it, the horse's legs was down near out of sight and Giles was holding his head. So I went back and got three or four more chaps and they got a cart and some faggots of wood and put the wood under him and so got him out.

'It wasn't only horses. I knew a person that went in. I helped get 'un out and I helped bury 'un. He was buried as the Lone Hiker. That happened up over Postbridge way. There was this farmer, Jack Donnelly, and he went up to see his sheep and he saw something white out across the bog and went over to see what it was. When he got out there he found a haversack.

'All he could see of the bloke was his feet from his knees, sticking up straight out of the bog. There was his two legs with his two hiking boots on. Donnelly he come back to Postbridge and got the police. I was in the Special Police then because of Dartmoor Prison and convicts escaping — because I joined the Special Police, the prison authorities put in a telephone for father. They put it in so I could go to Dartmeet Bridge and stop every cart or car and search 'un until the warders got there. In them days the warders only had horses or pushbikes and they'd 6 miles to come, by which time the man would be away. So it used to be my duty to do one night on and one night off, at the bridge with a warder, until they found the convict.

'Anyways, we got this young chap out of the bog and we buried him down to Princetown as the Lone Hiker since we didn't know who he was. The police took off his wristwatch and sent it to a jeweller and he found that the jeweller who had repaired it had put his mark inside the cover and so they found out from him that the young chap come from Warrington in Lancashire and we had to dig 'un up again and send 'un back to Warrington to be buried. He'd been in the bog above a fortnight before we dug 'un up, then by the time we buried him it was another month and then permission from the Home Office to take him up again, see. . . . He was hanging about for weeks one way or the other. He'd been making his way from Postbridge to Okehampton it turned out, straight way across the moor, he'd thought.

'Old George Smith over to Hexworthy once was up by old Hexworthy tin mine when he met two hikers going across the moor and he was a great old chap — Moor Man for the South Quarter — and he said, "where be you blokes off to?" and he said they were walking into Cornwall and he said, "you can't go across there, there's a blinking bog there if you get in, you won't come out again," and he tried to turn them back as they were going to walk through it, down one hill and up the next, but they just went on. I suppose they got through — we never heard nothing if they didn't.

'Anyone can get lost up on the moor. I did myself once. There was three of us coming back from a dance one night at Postbridge. Us was coming back along and 'twas thick with fog but we could see the light back at Penlee House, so back we went to Postbridge and thought we'd go back home a back way because there was a path. Anyroad, we set off and about 20 yards on from the path we saw this damn great big rock and I said, "what's here this rock? Darn it, he baint on the blooming path! So the path must be down here," I thought, so off us went again and blimey, there was that blinking rock again. We did that four or five times that night. Every time, we come back to that blinking rock. Us was still walking about when daylight come in and then we found our way back on the path. Now down near home they'd just opened up a big cesspit and it was just through a gate, right alongside the path. It was very slippery and there was old Stan Conford, darn me, if he didn't slip and fall in the cesspit. Golly, he stank! Well, the wind was in front of us and we were walking towards the wind, so we made old Stan walk behind us all.

'You learned the moor by knowing the different tors and crossing places. You got to know it like you'd know a town if you lived in 'un. You was safer then though 'cos it was all riding. If you got stuck in a thick fog, you just let the horse have its head and the horse would take you home. Always take you home they did. Fog did funny things to your sight — you'd see a pony 25 yards away and he'd look like a darn great carthorse. I'd a wonderful horse called Felix for years. It didn't matter where you was on the moor, he'd take you home.

'Dartmoor was wonderful hunting country too, best there was, because you could see so far. I used to hunt with the Dartmoor pack and the South Devon and Mid-Devon, all three packs. Dartmoor pack had the longest run there ever was — from Two Bridges they rode into Exeter country, right up near Exeter somewhere. There was never one fox, mind, there must have been more foxes. There was seventy horses started out and five of them got to the other end and I was one of them. That was about 1925. I nearly lost my life over that. I was coming down over from Laughter Tor down towards a place called Snails House and I come down there and the East Dart was in flood. Sid Piper was the whip and my great friend. Well, Miss Hall, she fell off on Laughter Tor and her mother came looking for her and I stopped and helped her and when I got down there they'd gone on. It was miles to the next bridge to cross over the river. Well those that were there, the horses wouldn't go in and the hounds wouldn't go in and George says, "come on, Jack, show them how to cross it," so us jumped into the blooming river and us come up yards down from where us went in, my horse was swept right down and I had to hang on to his back to get over to the other side. Old George followed me across but the others went up by Dunnabridge to get over. If the hounds hadn't run back a bit, I think we'd have been the only two left. . . .

'Then there was the convicts. People used to lock up their doors, see, when they knew one got out. It wasn't very often they got very far before they were caught. We'd 'un escaped twice and got to Exeter both times, chap name of Amey. They always picked them up.

'One night there was two warders on duty up Sherburton way and it was a miserable, wet sort of night and they was near a big old stone wall so they sat down behind the wall for a bit of shelter. Now this 'ere convict who'd got away from Princeton, he come across the moor see, he did think he was following the main road, but he'd followed a road off it but he thought if he kept the road in sight he'd know where he was to. It come in dark and they had bloodhounds out but they'd lost him when he crossed the River Swinkle. There was an old derelict house up Swinkle and they searched up there and couldn't find nothing so they called it off when it come in dark. Anyroad he wasn't all that far away, hiding in a bush. They had a little terrier with them and they didn't take no notice of him but he went up to the bush and he smoothed 'un down. He crept away over at Jones's house in the valley where he could see the lights. He was going to break in the house and it was this house wall these warders were sheltering behind. The convict he came down and climbed over right between the two warders. One of them catched 'un by the ankle.

'Then there was one escaped and got down to Roundhill Farm and hid in the loft and covered himself with hay. Now that was on the Sunday morning and he was going to hide out until Monday. Old Garner Oak's daughter, she went to the loft for some hay for the cows and sticked her fork in to him and he hollered out. He got out from under the hay and the maid she hollered for her father and he got his shot gun and come. It was only a mile and a half from the prison and in them days if you caught a prisoner they paid you £5. Old Garner Oak and his daughter, they marched 'un back up to the prison, Garner behind with the double-barrelled shot gun and they do say when they got up to the prison that old Garner wouldn't leave until the Governor gave him his £5.

'I knew everyone for miles. 'Twas different then to what it is today. Dammit they'd as soon cut your throat now. Us had no TV or wireless at first. The first whisker set came in 1922, the old cat's whisker with a crystal. We'd two earphones, Dad had one and I listened at the other and Mother, she ran between.

'During the winter us used to ride up to Shelverton or up to Zachariah Stevenson's and farmer Shaw's, up Shallowford, then up to Babery and we'd go out several nights a week and play cards and sing and have supper, then one night they'd come to us. We made our own fun on a winter's night like that.

'I left the farm in 1936. I'd got fed up with Dartmoor and came to Keinton Mandeville as a lorry driver. I'd really had enough of it in 1927 when we had the blizzard. We saw neither butcher, nor baker nor postman for six weeks. It started snowing on Christmas Eve. It was like the one in 1963. There was no snowploughs to clean the roads then — they used the unemployed and convicts, digging out the roads with shovels. Now Granfer he got took ill just before Christmas — he was 87. He had a little cottage at the back of the farm but we had him in the house in one of the bedrooms. We'd only oil lamps still up there so Father sent me over the Dartmeet to get paraffin. I think 2 gallons cost about 1s. I know if I went for 2 gallons of petrol with two bob I got the petrol and a packet of Woodbines. Anyroad on my way I had to cross Eight-Acre field, which was the short cut to Dartmeet to avoid the road.

We'd two carthorses in Eight-Acre.

'Well on the way back home across that field these two horses followed me and when I got to the gate, they pushed past me and knocked the gate out of my hand. They followed me back up the little lane and went into their stalls in the stable. I said to Father, "Derby and Darling have knocked the gate out of my hand and they're down in the stable." He said he couldn't understand it — the weather was mild, it had been raining all the day.

'Well there they were in their stalls and we couldn't get them out. We dragged and tugged and Father says in the end, it's Christmas night, leave them bide and we'll take them out tomorrow in the day. So Mother and Father went to bed and me and a chap called Charlie Gregory was sitting up with Granfer, taking it in turns to make up the fire. We'd a big open fireplace and come the early hours of the morning we needed more wood. Most of the wood we had was spruce which burned quickly. So I went and opened up the back door, or tried to, as it wouldn't open. I shoved and pushed and then it opens up — and there it was! We didn't know it had been snowing. All I could see was the print of the door in the height of the snow — the horses must have known.

'I couldn't get out of that door so I went round the front and opened that. There was a porch outside and the wind roaring heavens hard and as soon as I opened the door, it started to come in to the house, so we had to shut it. Then we all had to go out and dig our way to get the firewood and try and find the cows. We'd seven bullocks too, buried in one field and the snow came over the walls and hedges and buried the sheep under it. We was out all day. For six weeks we was carrying hay to the ponies and sheep and in those days you cut it all out with a hay knife. We had to take the hay up in a cart and tie it down with a pig net or it would all blow away.

'A few days after, Granfer died. We measured 'un and I and a friend walked to Princeton to the undertaker to ask him to make the coffin and to fix up things with the vicar. So he made the coffin and got some fellows from Princeton to carry it as far as Dunnabridge which was half way and then we went out and carried it back home. For the funeral about twenty of us carried it back, taking it in turns. We carried it on a long straight pole.

There were three men behind and three in front and the others carried lamps and we took him over the snow to Princeton graveyard where he was buried.

'Of course however bad the weather got you never ran out of food — flour, milk, butter, eggs you always had, of course. We had cider too. Every year father would buy up an orchard down Ashburton way and then we'd take the apples down to a farm where they had a cider press and take it home in barrels.

'We always killed a pig, too, the first week in November and salted 'un down. I couldn't understand when I come to Somerset the way they do salt down their pork. They do salt the pork dry, then they get the salt and rub it in and keep on rubbing it in. Us never did that. Us had what we called "trendles", like big earthenware pans, see, quite deep and sort of glazed inside. You would buy the salt in 28-pound blocks, two bob for 28 pounds it was. You used to put it in the copper in a drop of water and melt it down and let it cool, then we'd pack the pork in the trendles and pour the salt water over the top when it was cold.

'Then you'd pour 'un all off again and skim off the grease and reboil it all, take the pork out, pack it back in and pour the brine over it again and it would last you all the year. Then we'd take out the bacon and put it in muslin bags and hang it up from the ceiling on hooks — all the farms had bacon hanging on the ceilings in those days. Father used to go to other people and kill a pig, 2s. 6d. to kill a pig, and then go back next day and cut it up for a shilling.

'There was such old characters lived on the moor then. There was an old chap lived out near Princeton called Moses, Dick Moses. Now he drove a horse and cart for Halfyards, Halfyards were builders, and he had to take some cement and sand to a farm where some masons were doing some repairs.

'Now old Dick, he hated motors. Well, he'd got down to the bottom of Dartmeet hill and a bloke come along with his wife in a little motor, a model T Ford. Dartmeet hill is three-quarters of a mile or so up over and very steep at that. Old Dick he start up Dartmeet hill followed by the chap in the car and old Dick he stayed right there in the middle of the road, and the chap in the car had one of those old klaxons and he kept sounding it at Dick. Every now and then Dick would just stop and that meant the car had to stop too and to get going again the wife had to get out and find stones to put behind the wheels and the bloke he had to get out and swing the handle, there weren't no batteries then. They did this about four times going up Dartmeet hill. When they got to the top, Dick pulled in and the T Ford chap stopped and he got out and he was some hysterical and raging and Dick he said, "Look here, my man, don't you cuss me. The Lord Almighty sent that horse and cart into the world for the use of man, the Devil sent that thing into the world for to kill man" — and that's the truest words ever a man spoke.

'There are few people left now who know Dartmoor like I do. A man called George Dysart did two books, one was *A Day's Walk from Dartmeet*, and then we got friendly and used to have a drink or two in the Forest Inn and he said he wanted to do one on the Abbot's Way. Now the Abbot's Way used to run from Tavistock to Buckfastleigh and the old monks they'd marked it with crosses. So he walked it in two parts, 12 miles at a time, and then I rode the whole way one Sunday on horseback. When the monks came to a marshy place they would make a pathway over it with stones and put oak posts in to show where it was. In one place now there was only one oak post left, the others had rotted away. I wonder if anyone could find it now?

'He'd said to me he wanted some photographs of all the old stone crosses and I thought, "durn it, I've a camera." I only gave 3s. 6d. for it in a jumble sale over to Tavistock years ago and he's still upstairs. He took beautiful pictures. So when I rode the Abbot's Way that Sunday I took all the photographs and it says "photography by John Down" in the book.

'They're all going. Every year I do go up there and ask after old so-and-so and find he died last week or he died the week before. I went down the pub back home four or five years ago and one old chap was in there and I asked him about some of the people and all that and he kept saying the same thing, they'd all gone. The landlord was a stranger to the place and he didn't know anything about anyone when I asked him about this and that. Finally he said, "damn it all, man, how many more are you going to ask for that's dead?" .'

17

Brewing in a London village

Most of this book has dealt with dying trades and industries but there are still a few traditional ones which are flourishing. Brewing is one of the nation's oldest industries and what is fascinating is that it is the small breweries, using traditional methods, who have survived best over the last difficult years — those who did not sell out to the giant conglomerates, that is.

In the mid-nineteenth century, London apart from the city centre, was still a collection of villages loosely joined together and whole small communities were dependent upon one local industry. The Ram Brewery in Wandsworth was one such, owned since 1831 by the Young family, and it is still going strong today. It is a family business in which family employees work — Charlie Butler, who retired as head horsekeeper, held the job for forty-three years. The present head horsekeeper is only the third in a hundred years, the first, John Cornish, doing the job for sixty-seven years.

The brewery, which stands on the banks of the Wandle, goes back to 1675 and although Young's have brought in a number of modern devices, there is much still there which is old. Until recently the power came from two beam engines, one dating from 1846 and the other from 1867, and they still work well. Although present power comes from gas, the beam engines are kept on for use at any time. The beer still brewed in the old way, using malt, hops, sugar, yeast and water and nothing else. There is no waste – local pubs are supplied by horse drays and the manure goes back to the land for the hops. In the farmyard at the back of the brewery – unique in London – are geese which act as watchdogs. There is also a smithy and a farrier's to look after the horses. Even the spare yeast from the beer is made use of and goes to make Marmite.

Young's still draw many of their employees from the local people and those who have worked for the brewery retain a lifelong affection for it. Bill Freeman has now been retired for nine years. He and his family have moved to Dorset where, on a lovely sunny day, he sat in his garden against a wall on which there was a huge loganberry bush, heavy with fruit. He looked a picture of health, an excellent recommendation for drinking beer.

'I was born near Wimbledon although my mother's family came from Dorset, near Blandford, and that's why we came back this way. I started at Young's as a joiner but I ended up by working in just about every department in the place, spread over forty years. I've been trying to make a few notes recently though about my very earliest memories, such as remembering crickets on the hearth and straw being put down in the streets.

'When people who were well off were sick, they'd lay down straw in the road about 50 yards each side of their houses to quieten down the noise of the horses and carts with iron-shod wheels. It's funny but it really was noisy then.

'A little while ago an old chap near here who's about 90 said he'd like to go up to London and see Piccadilly where he used to work for some tobacco firm or other. Well, his son took him up and though they didn't recall him at the firm (it's actually still there) once they knew who he was and what he'd done they gave him a lunch and made a fuss of him and someone said, "I suppose you can see great changes." "Oh yes," he said, "it's so *quiet* now." They couldn't believe it. They looked out of the window at the streams of traffic and the dreadful noise. "You see," said the old boy, "in my day it was all cobbles and the horses and cabs were going up and down all the time with their iron wheels and horses hooves and the noise was deafening." He thought the traffic moved faster, too, with less jams!

'When I began at Young's, although a lot of the men who worked there weren't what you'd call educated by today's standards, they were real personalities. Now everybody seems the same. They were great on story telling and some of the old chaps in the brewery could recall what their fathers had told them it was like seventy or eighty years earlier so that you were going back a long time, well over a century. I really picked up the history of the area that way − some of the old houses on the edge of the brewery were Huguenot silk weavers' houses; they had quite a colony there. They were grand old chaps even if some of them were rogues and rascals.

'Now old Henry Young, he was chairman for fifty years, he was a real old Victorian gentleman and he treated his employees as servants − I remember once being introduced to some man who he was showing around the brewery and he actually said, "this is Mr Freeman, one of my servants." But he was very just, painfully honest − the biggest crime then was to tell a lie. If he caught you out being untruthful you'd be very, very unpopular indeed and you could be unpopular for a year. If it was really serious you'd get the sack; but if you told the truth, even if you had made a careless mistake, then you'd be forgiven. It's not like that now, of course, the unions would have something to say about it.

'We worked very long hours. The stokers came in first at 4 a.m. to start up the boilers − for the mash to be boiled. They'd start boiling up about 5 a.m. Then the brewery workers would arrive at 6 a.m., and we used to be given coffee and biscuits, coffee so thick you could stand the spoon up in it. Breakfast would be from eight until nine, lunch from one until two and you'd go home at 4.30 p.m.

'If you were five minutes late for work you were fined 3d., a quarter of an hour, 6d. After a quarter of an hour you were sent home until breakfast time and lost two hours' pay. That was quite a lot then − a craftsman got about £3. 15s. a week, a labourer £2. 10s. − and he could live on that. My first big money was £5 a week, I used to put some by for holidays, save a little bit, give some to the wife to spend as well as her housekeeping, and pay a mortgage too. It doesn't seem possible now but then everything was cheaper − cigarettes were 9d. for twenty and beer from 4d. to 6d. a pint. Sometimes

I would take the wife up to quite a posh restaurant in Rupert Street and get a good, four-course dinner for 7s. 6d. each., and they'd treat you like Lord Muck.

'The Youngs always tried to keep their employees on, even if sometimes they had to go on short time in the winter. There'd always be some men hanging around the gate hoping for work, they called them "the odd men", and they'd get taken on for days, or weeks or even two or three months. If they were good then they'd try to find them a regular job when one came up.

'There was real class distinction then though. The brewers and the office staff didn't have anything to do with the labourers and workers in the yard, they kept quite aloof. Mr John Young changed all that when he came in and took over. He said the man in the yard was just as important as the clerk in the office. After you'd been in the brewery a few years, he'd call you by your Christian name.

'They were always larking about practical joking then too. It was always taken in good humour. I think if you tried some of the things on now you'd finish up with a fight. I remember one man who bought some new boots and they took them out of his bag before he went home and substituted bricks and he walked home for miles carrying the bricks. Then they would play tricks on the night watchman like stringing up dead rats for him to walk into in the dark. Another trick was to nail somebody's boots or shoes down to the floor and one they tried on everyone was to bore a tiny pinhole in the bottom of the glass and watch them try to drink out of it.

'You got an allowance of 2 quarts of beer a day. I don't think they drink so much now because of the drink and drive laws but in my first days they either walked to work or came on trams so it didn't matter. You drew your beer allowance from an outside place which was known as "the fiddle" — I don't need to tell you why it was called that. . . .

'Young's still brew the old way, of course. At the top of the building the melted barley goes into the mash tuns, then the "liquor" is added - you can't mention the word "water" in brewing — then it goes on to the coppers where the liquid sugar goes in, and the hops, before passing on to the fermenting vessels where the yeast is added. It takes seven days to make a good brew and there's a superstition it must always lay over Sunday or it is an unGodly beer which has not been blessed by the Sabbath. After that, nowadays, it goes down either for barrelling or to the mechanical bottling plant.

'But there will always be something of a mystery about beer. There is a lot of art in breeding the yeast for instance — the first yeast off is the "dirty head", the next one then is a good yeast. This one they keep for other brewing, any other yeast — perhaps two or three more skimmings — is sold for products like Marmite. Bakers don't seem to want brewers' yeast much any more — at least the big ones don't. They seem to want chemically made yeasts.

'Although we made all our own yeast it could still mean problems. One source of trouble, especially in the springtime, was the appearance of "wild yeast". They discovered it was because of the direction of the prevailing winds, coming from the South Downs and passing over wild flowers, particularly gorse. The pollen would come down with the wind and produce the wild yeast and spoil the brew — you wouldn't think that could happen in central London would you? Wild yeast is a menace, although a good brewer can spot immediately if a beer isn't fermenting right. Young's always let their beer ferment properly and leave it until it has stopped. Some of the big brewers stop fermentation when they want to and often not all the starch has turned into sugar. A properly fermented beer is digestible, one that hasn't stopped is not.

'Obviously mechanisation has come in since my early days. Just take the bottling plant, for instance. It used to be done by bottling boys. First the bottles would be stuck by hand on to two revolving brushes to clean them inside. Then they'd be put on to the bottle-fill to fill them up, that was a revolving filler, then taken off by hand and laid on a 6 inch round tray and the labels were behind the bottles. The boy would pick them up two at a time, one in each hand, wipe them on some gummy stuff and then stick them on the bottles. Now a machine does it all — thousands of bottles an hour.

'I used to look after one machine myself because nobody else could understand it. It was called the ozone machine. It was invented by a Mr Clarke, a student of Wimshurst. It consisted of six 2-inch glass plates, each plate a quarter of an inch from its opposite one. Revolving in opposite directions were about thirty silver steel brushes, gloss-coated with shellac varnish. They could generate 25,000 volts — like a Wimshurst wheel. This passed on to an old-fashioned brush aerial in a 2-foot cube with glass panels with its inside covered with wire netting. Static electricity passed from the ends of the wire brushes to the earth wire netting, air then passed through the box, all bacteria were killed by the static electricity and the air then passed through wire sieves and three layers of butter muslin, then through a 6-foot tank with plates over which there were layers of glycerine. Any particles of dirt stuck on the glycerine. The air was pumped through the tank and out over the fermenting vessels, purified. . . . There you had it, one of the world's earliest air conditioning machines!

'Of course it was done away with in the end and the bits that weren't destroyed were stacked away in the yard. One day Mr Clarke's grandson, the inventor of the machine, came to ask what had happened to it and we gave him the bits and he reassembled it for a museum somewhere.

'Then there was coopering — that's very skilled. We used to use Russian oak for the barrels but that became unobtainable. The American oak wasn't as satisfactory and then we were not allowed to import it anyway because it might bring in American oak disease which would affect our own oak trees. The old barrels were just wood inside but later on they used to put a black oily substance in, spin the barrel around until the whole of the inside was coated, and then dry it with air jets. It was mainly for cleanliness, it made them easier to clean. As time went on it became harder to get the wood and make their own wooden barrels so they used to buy them up from other breweries which had either gone bust or stopped using them and cannibalise them to make good ones.

'A skilled cooper can make a barrel without ever using a rule — just a mark on a stick and a great deal of experience. He would never be more than a pint or so out. There's real beauty in an oak barrel. The timber is an inch and a half thick and no matter where it is kept the temperature of the beer will not alter a great deal — even if you stand it in the sun it will only go up a few degrees. In today's metal containers it would boil. They're very bad for the beer.

'Young's still have some of the old fermenting vessels made of wood. The new ones are metal and can be mechanically cleaned but all the old ones, wood lined with copper, had to be cleaned by hand — indeed those remaining still are. You would drop a candle in first to see how much CO_2 there was. If it went out you didn't get inside. If you breathed any of it in you'd be unconscious in seconds, and after a few minutes you'd be suffering from softening of the brain.

'The old boilers ran on coal, then oil and now it's gas. Steam was used throughout the brewery for boiling the coppers, heating the water, in all the departments. The barrels were cleaned with steam, then hot air blown through. A chap would poke a gas flame through the tap hole and look in the top to see if it was properly clean inside.

'I can't understand why they aren't still using the beam engines. They ran entirely on *waste* steam, each one on about 80 pounds of steam. The gearing of those engines is beautiful, mostly either ordinary cogs or mitred cogs and one wheel is cast steel and the other is steel with Hornbeam teeth. I was the only one in the brewery who could re-teeth the wheels, now there is nobody there who can do it. The beauty of the wooden teeth is that if you have an accident with your engine or just get it jammed up, it breaks away without destroying the engine or any other of the other parts.

'You talk about stone masonry being the oldest craft — I'd say it was brewing. The oldest and most diverse of all trades. You can't think of any other craft which hasn't been used in the brewing industry — stone for building, woodwork, carpentry, engineering — every branch of it — glass making, and now science and technology. It's all there. There's farming for the hops and barley, farriers and smiths for the horses.

'At least Young's have stayed with the horses — they're famous of course for showing shire horses. I understand even bigger breweries are going back to the horse — they're much more economical on short hauls. Young's reckon that on all 3 mile journies they absolutely pay for themselves. Up to 5 miles it is still economic, though you can probably only manage one journey a day instead of two. After that they use lorries but they deliver about 10,000 tons of beer a year by horse transport and their only outgoings are feed, chaff we called it; that and the work for the farrier. The shoes for the big dray horses take 2 foot of steel to make.

'There are a lot of traditions which still hang on in brewing. You know that they mark beer with Xs to show its strength? It doesn't mean as much as you think because different breweries use different measurements so one's XX might be much stronger than another's, for example, but they say it dates from the Middle Ages when a lot of the brewing was done in the monasteries. After the ale was matured the abbott would come round and sample the beer and declare it fit for sale and then bless it. After he'd blessed it, he'd chalk the sign of the cross on the barrel and over the years it became a tradition in brewing so they still used it although the sign of the cross became an X.'

Bill Freeman feels he has been fortunate to spend his life in a trade he loves.

'They realised it at the brewery and I became a kind of local historian for them and used to show VIPs around the brewery and tell them about it. I still have my links. I go up and see them all about once a month or so and when the Queen went around the brewery some time ago they invited me up to meet her.

'I miss drinking Young's down here, of course. You get used to your own beer. But about twice a year they send me a crate down so I keep in touch as it were. . . .'

BIBLIOGRAPHY

D.B. Barton, *Essays in Cornish Mining History* (D. Bradford Barton, Truro, Part I, 1968, Part II, 1970).

David Butcher, *The Driftermen* (Tops'l Books, Reading, 1979).
David Butcher, *The Trawlermen* (Tops'l Books, Reading, 1979).

Alfred Jenkins, *Gigs and Cutters of the Isles of Scilly* (published in Scilly, 1975).
Alfred Jenkins, *The Scillonian and his Boat* (Penwell, Truro, 1982).

A.K. Hamilton Jenkins, *Mines and Miners of Cornwall*: Parts 1 to 5 (Forge Books, Bracknell, between 1961 and 1969).

Jean Lindsay, *A History of the North Wales Slate Industry* (David & Charles, London and New York, 1974).

Raphael Samuel (ed.), *Miners, Quarrymen and Saltworkers* (Routledge & Kegan Paul, London, 1977).